ON PRAYER

ON PRAYER

by

Karl Rahner, S.J.

PAULIST PRESS DEUS BOOKS

NEW YORK   PARAMUS   TORONTO   LONDON

A Deus Book Edition of Paulist Press, 1968, by special arrangement with Clonmore & Reynolds, Ltd.

NIHIL OBSTAT:
Joannes O'Donoghue
Censor Theol. Dep.

IMPRIMATUR:
✠ Joannes Carolus
Archiep. Dublinen. Hiberniae Primas

July MCMLXVII

The Nihil Obstat and Imprimatur are official declarations that a book or pamphlet is free of doctrinal or moral error. No implication is contained therein that those who have granted the Nihil Obstat and Imprimatur agree with the contents, opinions or statements expressed.

Copyright © 1958 by
Clonmore & Reynolds, Ltd.

Cover Design: Morris Berman

Published by Paulist Press
Editorial Office: 304 W. 58th St., N.Y., N.Y. 10019
Business Office: Paramus, New Jersey 07652

Manufactured in the
United States of America
by Our Sunday Visitor Press

CONTENTS

THOU WILT OPEN MY HEART.

THE life of men is made up of many and varied activities. Deep in the heart of men is the longing, fitfully glimpsed and but half realised, to gather up all these strivings into an intense pursuit of one all-embracing objective worthy of the toil and tears and devotion of the human heart. Such is the half-shaped dream; but the reality is a picture of heaped-up activities, where the trivial jostles the less trivial, and the less trivial elbows the important things, and there is no unity of design, nor any intensity of single, concentrated purpose. There is no real perspective of values: what is essentially trivial but immediately urgent, looms large and commands attention; while what is essentially important, but not immediately urgent or insistent, is relegated to the hazy recesses of the background. But the thing of greatest importance is not always what is demanded by the needs of the moment.

A man may turn from it all; and immediately the noise of his activities sinks to silence as, in a spirit of reverence and love, he speaks to God in prayer. With one swift upward glance of his soul, he has got as near as his finite nature will allow him, to that sublime fusion of all his activities into one glowing point of heat and of light. Only in Heaven can he fully achieve this synthesis of all his faculties, of all the energies of his being, in the contemplation of the Beatific Vision. Here on earth, hedged in by the things of the senses, such synthesis is impossible to men; and yet, in prayer, though " through a glass in a dark manner ", a man looks upon God and comes as near as he can to that unity of action and purpose for which his heart has a deep and secret longing. Prayer is, therefore, one of the essentials of our life—the food we feed to our souls in order that this deep and secret longing may live into eternal life.

But there is no compulsion to pray: we can freely decide to pray or to neglect prayer. When we say that prayer is necessary, we mean necessary for the highest part of man's nature; and just as the highest part of man—his soul—is often ignored, so too is prayer. For prayer is not easy. It is not the speaking of many words, or the hypnotic spell of the recited formula; it is the raising of the heart and mind to God in constantly renewed acts of love. We must go forward to grapple with prayer, as Jacob wrestled with the angel. We must lift high our lamp of Faith that it may show us what prayer is, and what are its power and dignity. Into the darkness we must whisper our prayer: *Lord, teach us how to pray.*

The idea is sometimes entertained that we know what prayer is, that we know how to pray, and that therefore we have simply to put our knowledge into practice. However, like so many other ideas which we regard as ordinary currency of knowledge—ideas about the nature of kindness, generosity, charity, silence, understanding, and so forth—our ideas of what prayer is and how we should pray are far from clear. We must question those ideas and thereby come to realize that, so far from the idea of prayer being something which leaps to us spontaneously from the front line of obvious ideas, it is a concept which it will take us our whole life to fathom, and a practice which our whole life will be too short to perfect.

We speak for our times: there probably was an era when the knowledge and practice of prayer were more familiar to men. There was almost certainly a time when men's spiritual arteries were less hardened; for instance, the very trowels and hods of the builders of Chartres Cathedral must have prayed, for the hands holding them were speaking a prayer in stone. But our spiritual climate has changed, and we have become spiritually hardened. The process has been a slow one, each generation inheriting the hardness and spiritual insensitivity of its predecessor, to hand it on to its successor as a legacy of yet greater hardness and spiritual insensitivity But the tradition of prayer has come down to us, and we give it some frigid respect. Prayer lives among us as the wraith of what it was. It lives on bored and casual lips that know nothing of prayer as earth's hymn of praise. Dry hearts offer their dry homage; eyes flit constantly to a watch which ticks its way towards the time of that really important appointment. God will understand and excuse this somewhat prefunctory discharge of one's spiritual duties; there are so many important things to be done. So God receives a crust of worship served distractedly on an ill-washed plate. But He has His honourable place in our scheme of things. We call on Him as we would to our insurance office; we pay grudgingly and we seek eagerly for our bonus. Our hands outstretched in prayer are mercenary hands; they show a certain near-parody of spiritual eagerness only when we are asking for something. This, of course, though witnessing to that hardening of the spiritual arteries we spoke of, is better than complete spiritual sclerosis. But what a travesty of prayer it really is! It is surely but the odour of an empty vase.

What, then, is prayer? We shall see that it is by no means easy to answer this question. When we have said all that is in our minds about prayer, it is inevitably found that we have said a lot *about* prayer and yet very little about what prayer *is*. Let us begin with one simple fact, so often regarded as a spiritual cliché that we tend to pass too lightly over it. Prayer is the opening of the heart to God. To understand this primary condition of prayer, both as a fact and as a reality to be lived, it is necessary to consider what precisely is meant by " the opening of the heart ", and what are the obstacles to this opening.

It is a well established psychological fact that actions deliberately and consciously performed are motivated by unconscious urges, are controlled by emotions long buried in the recesses of our being; so that, what appear to be actions done in the full light of consciousness, are but the shadows and symbols of buried urges which now suddenly become active beyond the reach of our conscious will. What appeared, therefore, as straightforward acts consciously controlled, are shown to be, as it were, a mirror held up to the true inner reality of ourselves. Thus we come to realise, with a rush of panic, that what we regard as actions posited by us are in reality but aspects of our real selves: they are *us*.

Let us try to further this idea by means of an analogy. Many of us remember those long nights in an air-raid shelter during the war, when we stood in abysmal loneliness among a crowd of terror-stricken people, waiting for death. In the darkness, we felt the coldness of fear chilling our hearts, and it was in vain that we put up a show of courage and stiff upper lip: our brave words were hollow, and fell as husks about our feet, leaving only silence and the vigil that might be the vigil of death. Then suddenly the explosion came, and the shower of débris to bury us. Let this be taken as the symbol of modern life. We have indeed crawled out from the powdered shelters; we have resumed our daily lives with a great show of bravery and pretence of enjoyment; but the truth is that many of us are as though we had remained buried in the débris, because we have suffered no change of heart through having been brushed by the wing of death. However far fetched it may sound, it remains true that externals are but the shadow of what has taken place in the depths of our hearts. Our hearts are obstructed, buried under débris.

Let us be quite clear about one fundamental fact of human existence. Unless it is set free by God into that infinite freedom wherein alone it can realise itself, our heart becomes hedged in by mean limitations, by suffering, by hopelessness, by the daily commonplaces that chain us down. Like the insatiable cormorant, the human heart then begins to feed upon itself. It becomes a welter of vanities, a sour well of bitterness and despair, a prison from which there is no escape. We may seek to escape by travel—forgetting the warning that "one may change the sky overhead, but not the mind within"; we may seek oblivious immersion in work or in that sick unrest that is miscalled pleasure; we may seek to stifle our loneliness amid the laughter of men. But there is no escape from that ceaselessly nagging sense of utter loneliness and of helpless conviction that the world is futile. We know that we are in hectic flight from ourselves; that we cannot stand still for a moment because the voices within us will say we have not moved at all—that we are still in the puddle of futility. We are like a person who appears to be in good health, but is really being gnawed by an incurable disease. A little stab of pain suddenly coming in the midst of enjoyment, reminds such a person that all this is mere pretence and that he is shadowed by death.

We may choose any form of escapism dictated by our

taste for pleasure and by the limits of our resources; we may build our house of happiness with what bricks we choose, or wander at large to gather the roses of pleasure. Yet, at a thought, the shades of our prison house are again stiflingly about us: we realise that we have but crawled from the misery of one cell to that of another— or, to revert to our metaphor, we have simply hollowed out another place in the same débris. Filling our lives is the same futility, frustration, monotony, chatter and all that weary swirl of pointless strivings we call human life. There are many, of course, who sit contentedly in the dust, feasting on the store they have, conversing brilliantly with their neighbours, still rooting for the truffles of pleasure, still dreaming and planning, apparently oblivious of the fact that the shelter has collapsed and that there are tons of débris between them and the light. Yet, even such hide-bound optimists, with their blinkered minds, will suddenly be jolted into the realisation that they are breathing the dust, that there is death in the air, and bitterness in the dregs of life's pleasures.

But in the dust of the powdered shelter, there are also the stoics who claim to know that the position is hopeless, and who stand up to proclaim this barren truth; who lift up the lamp only to show that there is really nothing but dryness and despair. They speak sternly to the poor wretch who shudders from them, in the icy grip of his sudden realisation that he is utterly alone, that his diet must be dust, that there is nothing beyond the inevitable blow of death. They tell him he must learn self-control by facing calmly up to the fact that there is no escape, and the poor wretch accepts this state of stultifying despair so that he comes to accept it as the ordained order of things. He is convinced that there can be no other state, that he has awakened from the illusions of life, that he has put aside like the toys of his childhood those dreams and ideals with which he used to feed his soul. He has experienced his bitter epiphany of despair.

Those who have settled down to this chronic despair preserve their self-control, appear to be leading—and regard themselves as leading—a perfectly natural life. They behave reasonably, work conscientiously, observe standards of decency, marry, found a settled home, discuss the arts and sciences. Occasionally they like to indulge in a little speculation about the meaning and value of human life, or to listen to such speculation. But all this is a mere façade to conceal the real man—to hide that wound from which the heart is bleeding to spiritual death, but about which one may not speak because it is "bad form" to indulge in what one of their number has once called "spiritual nudism". All this is a mere pretence at ignoring the prison whose exit is blocked by the débris of their own hearts. Within that prison, their real self is hopelessly trapped—that self which does not wear the spectacles of humanist sophistication, that raw self which sees unerringly into the hollow heart of earthly life, and judges it to be empty, futile and subject to death.

Modern philosophy has invented a new and flattering mask for the countenance of despair. Man's true dignity, it says, is to realise that there is nothing beyond the material things around him, that he himself is no more intrinsically permanent than the trees and the grass "that today is and tomorrow is cast into the oven", that human life has no more meaning than is summed up in the terrible words: "from day to day we ripe and ripe, and from day to day we rot and rot". There is no true human dignity except that of facing up calmly and bravely to the absolute worthlessness of human existence. A man's wisdom is to be measured by his realisation of his own utter lack of any significance. This so-called philosophy of despair has been formulated by one such philosopher as "an icy silence in face of the eternal silence of the alleged Divine"; and the same author (Camus) claims for this philosophy that it establishes "a meaningless and godless world which thinks clearly and which no longer hopes".

There is, of course, a certain *positive* realisation of one's fundamental nothingness which may be the beginning of salvation: "of myself, I can do nothing" said Saint Paul: and those who have come to such a realization may be already close to establishing the kingdom of God in their hearts. The philosophical despair of which we have spoken above, is simply perverted pride: it is as though a man should say—"I shall calmly despise my whole existence because it does not make me a god ". Such a man comes to take pride in his realisation of his very worthlessness, as though it were a positive achievement which gave him dignity. " Greatness has changed its field: it is now to be looked for in resoluteness and sacrifice without hope", writes Camus. What a parody of human life we have here, in this picture of man's finest qualities being exercised in an affirmation of worthlessness and sheer negation! The head remains " bloody but unbowed ", and the eyes look forward unflinchingly to where there is no hope, no destiny, no line of light rimming the eternal hills. How different is the positive sense of its own nothingness characteristic of the truly Christian soul! For this realization is simply a measuring of ourselves against the greatness of our Creator, and a casting out of all that is petty and earthly in us so that we may remove all obstacles to the indwelling of the strength of God in our bodies chosen by Him to be His " temples ". It was from a realisation—a positive, fruitful realisation—of his own nothingness and worthlessness, that Saint Paul made his magnificent boast: " I can do all things in him that strengtheneth me." It is a great paradox to those who have not the eyes of faith, that such abasement and such audacity can exist together, almost as cause and effect, in the Christian soul.

Stripped of its mask of sophism, this philosophical despair is revealed as mere negativity—as ordinary, barren despair dressed in fine feathers. Behind the words and the lofty protestations of the modern philosophers, there is simply emptiness and frantic self-deception. They are like those deceptive ruins one sometimes sees, where a sound façade, viewed from a distance, gives the illusion of a house standing four-square and solid; but, viewed at nearer range, is revealed as an empty shell housing only heaps of the débris that once were roof and walls and windows open to the light. But such philosophers claim to stand upright in the heart of this shell, boldly denying the existence of those heaps of débris because they assert that the roof and the walls were mere illusions; and yet, under that débris, are buried their true freedom, their faith, their hope of an eternal destiny, for they have never learned the secret of the freedom of the adopted sons of God.

Even the Christian must be on his guard lest his own house has crumbled to some extent, and some of his true greatness been buried under its débris. The façade here will take the form of a dry discharging of prescribed duties wherein the heart has long ceased to play a living role. The danger of such crumbling is that it happens with great silence: it is rather a process of noiseless dry rot than such a fall of masonry as would jolt the attention. Thus the débris will silently gather; and mere observance of the externals of religious practices will not save the living reality of religion from becoming choked and buried beneath it.

A true realisation of one's worthlessness is fruitful and positive, because it is a realisation that what is subject to death in us is unworthy of claiming the allegiance of our hearts. It is the realisation that the most carefully planned projects, the most lofty ideals, the most impassioned strivings, are meaningless except as inspired by, and directed towards, the Eternal Power in Whom alone we "live and move and have our being". This is the conviction which enables a Christian to delve deeper and deeper into the realisation of his own nothingness and helplessness, because only thus can the power of God live in him. It was this truth that Christ put so vividly when He said: "Unless the seed falling into the ground die, itself remaineth alone; but if it die, it bringeth forth fruit". It is in the darkness of one's knowledge of complete personal worthlessness that the light of the presence of God begins to dawn: it is in the realisation of one's own utter powerlessness that the power of God becomes active, springing up into Life Everlasting.

Thoughts such as these should inspire the Christian who has allowed his soul to become filled with noise and bustle, to realise that God is awaiting the silence of his heart so that He may speak His word of power. He is awaiting that moment when the Christian ceases to spin fine words as a cloak for inner emptiness, to heap up dry prayer and arid observance of externals, to listen to the heart's moan of despair at the burden of life; for in that moment, He knows that the Christian will turn and say: "My existence has no meaning except as the manifestation of Thy Power and Glory through my weakness and nothingness." The soul then realises the truth of the words that " he who will save his life must lose it "—that obsessive anxiety for happiness in this world leads only to the hovel of despair, not to the palace of wisdom. Every day becomes a renewed miracle, wherein the soul grows in deeper knowledge of its own powerlessness, and knows the growing power of God within the depths of its being. What once seemed a sterile sense of utter emptiness, proves to be but the greyness before the dawn of Grace in the soul. The heart is buried in the sense of its own futility, but there is no need to seek an exit of escape, because God is present. It would be fatal to turn from this blessed realisation of one's loneliness and futility, to seek comfort from things that have no power to comfort us, because they are but shards that can hold no water. In a fresh affirmation of faith and love, the soul must descend deeply into the knowledge of its own worthlessness, for only by doing so can it find God. It is not *despite* the fact of our nothingness that we find God, but *because* of our realisation that we are as nothing in His sight and that the world is dust and ashes except as the means of loving and serving Him. Deep cries unto deep: the depth of our nothingness unto the depth of the power and majesty and wisdom of God.

With this new awareness of God, comes deep and lasting peace—a calm which is not deceptive, a confidence without fear, a security that needs no reassurance, a power that lives in powerlessness, a life that springs up in the shadow of death. Nothing is left in us but God and our faith in God. We find our happiness, our strength, our power to face all sorrow, in the thought that God is with us and that we are His. In this peace, our heart learns to commune silently with God in a living union with Him. The dry formulas of prayer on dry lips, are replaced by that silent communion of heart with heart which comes with the sense of God's nearness to us and our utter, loving dependence on Him. This colloquy of the heart with God cannot be expressed in words, because it is a silent reaching out towards God with reverential fear and sublime trust. It is a complete silent oblation of self, and an entire surrender to God.

And here again we come upon one of the exalted

mysteries of the spiritual life. In thus abandoning himself to God, the Chrisitan can cry out with Saint Paul: "I live, now not I, but Christ liveth in me"—because the pulsating centre of his life has ceased to be other than the Life and Power of God dwelling within him. Yet, by a splendid paradox, it can be said that in ceasing to be himself the centre of his life, he becomes more entirely at one with himself; because God is more the true centre of our being that we are ourselves. The sheer Immensity of God urges us to realise our being to its fullest through transcending the limitations imposed by choosing to remain our own centre. For we now know that within those limitations there is no salvation, but only emptiness and frustration. The darker and more difficult the ways leading to this peace, the more intense is the love in hearts that have sought refuge from the threat of God's judgments by sweet submission to God Himself. Peace has come because the heart has opened to admit the presence of God, saying: "O God of my heart, and the God that is my portion forever. Abba, father. Have mercy on us." The Christian surrenders unconditionally, listens to the inspirations of God now breathing their power within him, filling him with a reverence and awe wherein is the healing power of eternal love. In this new freedom from thraldom to self, every word and act becomes a lived prayer, because the presence of God suffuses the whole pattern of living. Here is real prayer: here is the Power of God set free at last to spring up in the acknowledged barrenness of the human heart.

To reach this blessed state of peace of soul demands an initial step into the unknown, and therefore a decision which must be freely taken and which cannot be imposed. A man may cling to his philosophy of despair, his creed of life's utter meaninglessness, as a drowning man clings to a plank; and it is as little use to tell him that he can relinquish this philosophy and yet find happiness, as it is to impress on the drowning man that he should release his hold, that he really can swim, when he is convinced that he cannot and that he will undoubtedly drown. As long as he clings to the plank, he cannot put this assurance to the test, and must float aimlessly; for he wants, not an assurance that he can swim, but almost an advance guarantee that the water itself will bear him up. But no such guarantee can be given. So, too, a man may look for such an impossible guarantee before he relinquishes his philosophy of despair by praying; and yet, he must take the initial step of laying aside this paralysing anxiety. If he feels himself incapable of praying, he must nevertheless kneel, join his hands, speak words of prayer even if he feels that these words come only from his lips and that his heart remains unmoved. For such a conviction as to the insincerity of his prayer may be the last defence offered by his philosophy of despair against inevitable defeat. " I believe, Lord: help Thou my unbelief", must be his prayer; and there is nothing insincere in such a humble admission of one's weakness of faith and one's difficulty in believing.

It is vain to plead inability, for in this matter, 'inability' is simply an excuse for making no effort. There is no inability preventing this decision, and one's greatest guilt may be to acquiesce in the idea that one cannot decide. But the ways of God are inscrutable; for if a man really longs for the strength to decide, and realises but is not obsessed by his own weakness, it is through that very weakness that God will work his salvation. Why should you not kneel, join your hands, speak the words of prayer, even when you feel that your heart is not in what you are doing? Is it the fear of insincerity? Is it insincerity to do what you feel you can do—force the body at least to do what you feel the heart cannot achieve but yet desires? You have got no right to stifle those longings deep within you for the possession of a key to the true meaning, the happiness, the exhilarating truth of life in God. The very fact that you repeat with such anguish: " I cannot do it," is already an admission that this is something longed for as good, and indeed an acknowledgement of a duty to seek this good. Your own free decision and your acting upon it will open the way to grace, but you cannot expect grace to come unsought. You cannot command the feelings of your heart. True; but there is one thing you can do. You can kneel down and tell God that your heart is dry and hard, but yet longs for Him. You can force yourself to pray.

In His Passion and Death, Christ has shown us how

the sense of being abandoned by God can be the dawn of God's presence in our dried and wearied hearts. For in this, as in every other aspect of our life, Christ has shown us how we must act by Himself undergoing the same desolation in His Heart for us and for our guidance. The Garden of Olives was the desolation of Christ in order that it might become the consolation of all human desolation, for Christ is the living heart of the world. Christ crushed to the earth, His sweat becoming as drops of blood trickling down unto the ground, His whole human nature shrinking from the agony upon which He had entered, is the God-Man forcing Himself to make a human prayer. In the silence of the Garden, Christ knelt alone, His whole being filled with the darkness of a seeming abandonment by the Father. Yet, overcoming the shrinking fear of His human nature, and with immense courage, He prayed: "Not my will but thine be done."

In that moment, all the desolation of the world, all the emptiness of human hearts, was lifted up and sanctified through Christ. We attain to profound union with God by uniting ourselves in our desolation with the Agony of Christ. He is the Way. "Thou wast walking in thy ways, a vagabond," writes Saint Augustine; "straying through wooded places, through rough places, torn in all thy limbs. Thou wast seeking a home, that is, a sort of settlement of thy spirit, where thou mightest say, it is well; and might say this in security, at rest from all uneasiness, from every trial, in a word from every captivity; and thou didst not find it. What shall I say? Did one come to show thee the way? There came to thee *the Way itself* . . ." (In Ps. LXX, Serm. ii, 3—Przywara p. 199). Our prayer in union with the agonizing Christ is a prayer of pure faith, and in the words which we struggle to say, we shall find His strength beginning to live in us. We shall receive grace to grow in holiness of heart unto ripeness for Heaven, because we have learned to unite our darkness with the desolation of Christ. "My pain cometh," writes Saint Augustine, "there will come my rest also; my trouble cometh, there will come my purgation also." (In Ps. LXI, 11—Przywara p. 469).

We have said very little in this chapter about prayer itself, but we have made an approach to the subject and, we hope, given an impulse also. We must try to develop a facility in opening our hearts to God, so that it may become a living reality in our prayer, and we may descend fruitfully into the depths of our heart, rather than deceive ourselves with a spurious philosophy of stiff-lipped despair. We must find courage by facing squarely up to the fact that there can be no complete rest for the soul, but rather disillusionment and bitterness, in the things whose end is the abyss of death. For deep in our hearts there is a profound restlessness, because God has given us a thirst for the Infinite, for the Incomprehensible, for Himself: "Thou hast made us for Thyself, O Lord," cried out Saint Augustine, "and our heart is restless until it rests in Thee." Deep in our buried heart, we find this seed of the Divine, this restless reaching out towards something infinitely beyond the things of this world; and we find strength to pray:

Our Father Who art in the depths of my heart, transforming its hollow emptiness into a heaven on earth; *Hallowed be Thy Name,* even in the death-like silence of my ignorance and my lack of faith; *Thy Kingdom come* in the very midst of my desolation; *Thy will be done* in me, even if it means pain and death; *Thy will be done* in me, for Thy will is my true life; *Give us this day our daily bread,* for I am utterly dependent upon Thy Divine Providence; *Forgive us our trespasses*—those sins which are ultimately but treason against Thy love for us, and therefore treason against myself; *Deliver us from evil*—from the evil of centering our lives upon ourselves, in order that we may learn that Thou art the centre of all, and that only in Thee can we find freedom worthy of the sons of God.

Perhaps, indeed, we may not really use so many words; but as we repeat the words of the Lord's Prayer, God will open our hearts that the warmth of these feelings may steal into the hard and stony places made arid by the bitterness of life.

II.

THE HOLY GHOST IN OUR PRAYER.

ONCE we have opened our hearts, we no longer seek to escape from ourselves; and where we formerly experienced an aridity empty of God, we now feel the joy of His Presence. In the depths of our heart we find the courage to say: " Our Father." We would never have the audacity, of our own accord, to address our Creator with such familiarity. Whence, therefore, do we derive the courage and the right to approach our Creator and speak to Him as His sons?

One thing in particular fills us with confidence: we speak these words in union with the Divine Son, Our Lord Jesus Christ. Christ adores the Father ' in spirit and in truth,' being born of the Father from all eternity. As God made man, Christ has adopted us as His brothers and co-heirs to His glory in the bosom of the Father; and that we may realise the full significance of that adoption, He teaches us to join with Him in saying: " Our Father." This prayer is the spirit of the New Law of Love proclaimed by Christ. No longer are we to look on God as the Almighty Judge and know nothing of His love for men. In Christ we have seen that love incarnate, and in the strength of that love we dare to say—*audemus dicere*—" Our Father". There is God and there are ourselves; and between us and God there is the stretch of infinity which our minds can never grasp. God, the all-Perfect, the all-Sufficient, the all-Holy; we, hanging by a thread of the mercy of God, utterly dependent on Him, dust in His sight. Only through Christ and at the bidding of Christ could men find the audacity to speak thus to God from the abyss of their own nothingness.

The Incarnation is our great source of inspiration in prayer. " In stooping without defiling Himself," wrote the famous seventeenth century mystic, Cardinal Berulle, " God the Son raises us; in His union with the Father, He purifies us; in Incarnating Himself, He deifies us . . ."

By assuming our nature, Christ became one of us in all things, sin alone excepted. In the bosom of His Father, He worshipped God from all eternity; and when He was made man, He worshipped with human lips and human thoughts. He invites us to join with Him in that worship, and by that invitation, by the sublime words in which He adopted us as His brothers, He swept away the cold fear which makes the creature crouch low in its own dust silent before the majesty of God or speaking only some trembling words of fear. Through Christ, men found a new dignity—that dignity which St. Paul flung as a magnificent challenge to the early Christians : " For know ye not that ye are the sons of God, and if sons, heirs also; heirs indeed of God and joint-heirs with Christ." We are no longer afraid—no longer dumb with the sense of our nothingness. We accept it, and the more intense our knowledge of the unapproachable majesty of God the greater our exaltation in accepting Christ's invitation to join our prayer with His and to say " Our Father ". We find the strength to pray through the realization that we do not pray alone, but " through Jesus Christ Our Lord " in union with the Church, His Mystical Body.

But our prayer must also be inspired by the Holy Spirit, the Third Person of the Blessed Trinity. Let us consider this more closely. We must find a place in our lives for the Holy Spirit, that this Spirit may pray in us and with us. There is a craving for the divine deeply stamped in our nature, whether we acknowledge it, or choke it with sin and worldliness; there is a divine discontent in us which made St. Augustine cry out: " Thou hast made us for Thyself, O Lord, and our hearts are restless until they rest in Thee." Only when the gates of our life are flung wide to the Spirit of God can this discontent be allayed; only when our souls become living temples of the Holy Spirit can that rest be ours.

We are the heirs to the ages, and we have inherited a strange confusion. Within the past few decades, there has been a craving for untrammelled freedom, because men will tolerate only such restraints as they choose to impose on themselves. This is the result of several centuries of spiritual lawlessness, in which men have ' progressively ' flung from them the authority of the Church, state, custom, tradition, in the name of what they called the "chainless spirit" of Man. Men claimed to be masters of their fate and captains of their soul. 'Freedom' became synonymous with true manhood; and so we invented free science, free love, *laissez faire* economy, free thought, free press, free expression, and a thousand other freedoms which we fondly imagined were adding cubit upon cubit to our human stature. There were moments of sublime, even if myopic, greatness in that struggle for freedom; there were far more frequent moments in which it was merely stupid rebellion against all restraint, an unworthy thirst for license and lawlessness. But men were so busy crying Freedom up and down the highways of life, that they had not perception to see that they were forging for themselves a new slavery. This was not an external slavery, as symbolised in the figure of the Dictator with his iron heel on the necks of a whole nation, and the smoking crematoria of his concentration camps as the sign of his power; nor was it even the slavery of poverty and hunger in the aftermath of war. It was an internal slavery, a chaining of the minds of men with fetters forged by themselves. Lust, ambition, greed and covetousness took command within the souls of men, in the places that had been swept clear of all hoary authority in the name of Freedom.

" See how kindred murder kin:
'Tis the vintage-time for death and sin:
Blood, like new wine, bubbles within:
Till Despair smothers
The struggling world, which slaves and tyrants win."

Men became slaves to the tyranny of their own passions, and began to reap the dry and withered harvest of their own despair. Life became meaningless, and the hearts of men were weary and dry of hope. Every man was free to be his own slave, and to live a life that was a miserable parody of the sublime freedom of a child of God for which he had been destined from eternity.

In the Middle Ages—the ages of Faith—men lived with their knowledge that God and eternity were waiting beyond the rim of human life; and that the greatness of man should be measured in the light of that fact. With the Renaissance and the Reformation, however, men lowered their eyes from the rim of life edged with eternity, and thought they could find a new freedom by making man the measure of man. The word 'man' itself was promoted to the dignity of a capital letter: the proper study of mankind was to be Man in all his dignity and freedom, sufficient unto himself, seeing only with his own eyes, believing only what was approved as 'rational' by his own mind. He began to take himself very seriously: he was 'rational' and he must fling wide human horizons before him, he must live fully, he must love passionately, he must follow knowledge like a sinking star, he must pass on the burning torch of human freedom undimmed. Science, art and poetry sought to fathom the secrets of life, "brooding over the dark abyss intent to hear its voices," as one poet said. The French Revolution enthroned beautiful women as Goddesses of Reason on the very altars of Catholic churches, heaped flowers in their honour, burned incense in their homage. In its very excess, this was a true picture of how men were turning in on themselves in a kind of worship of their own natures. And yet, the final result of all this was that the idea of Man became debased. No longer was he a being of great personal dignity, but simply a collection of atoms flung together fortuitously, a mere conduit by which the 'Life Force' passed from one generation to the next. He became the plaything of blind and ruthless forces; he saw himself as a cork tossed aimlessly on a dark ocean he could not fathom. He himself had little real and vital personality, because he had lost the answer to "the heavy and the weary weight of all this unintelligible world."

But the grip of materialism on the thoughts of men was loosened, in our century, by the developments in Psychoanalysis and Depth Psychology. Nineteenth century materialism had swept into oblivion all mysticism and all metaphysics, as outmoded ideas from a pre-scientific age. The province of the human mind was to be all knowledge, and mysteries had no place in it because mysteries could not be expressed in those clear scientific concepts which had become the new intellectual gods of men. There were, of course, strange irrational stirrings and cravings in men's souls, but these would be met by the new panacea—enlightenment. Morality was to be a matter of what was cricket and was was not cricket, assisted by a traditional behaviour; and, of course, an excellent police system was to be the guardian of good order. With the coming of Freud, however, men suddenly realized that they were living complacently in a half-world; that within themselves was another strange world full of blind forces and imperious instincts—the world of the unconscious, of whose very existence men had been unaware, and which they now found to fit very uneasily into the categories of materialism. The era of psychoanalysis had come, and the non-material element in man could no longer be ignored. Men became more and more aware that the springs of motivation and activity, which they had claimed to explain rationally, were in reality the expression of strange laws in an irrational and disturbing part of themselves. They groped into the newly discovered country of the unconscious, questioning its mysteries, gathering some vague answers; they became aware of it as a region where neat and satisfying 'clear scientific concepts' had no place, but where realities were but the prelude to greater realities, horizons suddenly swallowed up in greater horizons. It had been claimed that man was the measure of all things; and now men experienced a bitter awakening to the fact that they could not measure themselves nor fathom their own being.

The result of all this was that men lost any clear conception of what is their own nature, and what the aim and purpose of that nature. Now a complete mystery to themselves, men saw their neat and trimmed ideas degenerating into a writhing coil of cravings and blind possibilities. Which of these cravings expressed the real essence of Man? To which of the forces in their nature were men to abandon themselves? Were they to abandon themselves, in a spirit of Nietzschean *amor fati*, to lust or greed, to humanism or selfishness, to omniscient but barren intelligence, to intense living in the conviction that the grave takes all? Should men take up an attitude towards their own lives, or just drift with the current of experience and of pleasure? But by drifting, do not men miss the whole meaning of their existence, by shirking a decision? In the face of the new chaos suddenly revealed within their own nature, men could take the way of determination and decisive action. These glimpses of strange infinities within us are pointers to a thirst for Infinity, for God, which has been placed by our Creator in the very depths of our nature. We must not seize on these infinities—these "magic casements opening" into the recesses of our being—as idols to be enthroned in our lives. Their very multiplicity would only increase that modern disease we have called *Angst* and which is a vague dread accompanying the apprehension of freedom and limitless possibilities, but without a definite object. The far flung horizons within us must lead us to the Infinity of God, if we are to find peace and rest.

Where does God enter into all this? The first question that suggests itself is whether experience can reveal everything in the limitlessness of the soul. Has God been discovered among the infinities of the soul? Or has all this groping into the depths of the soul been a mere unearthing of rubble, of cheap and valueless knowledge, while the image of God revealed in these infinities has remained undiscovered? To answer these questions, we must turn to the Word of God. There is indeed something more in our souls than can be revealed by daily experience, by modern psychiatry or psychology, by mystical communion with nature, by the exaltation of art or of love—in short, by any attempts of the human mind to grasp infinity. All such fail to reach the ultimate meaning of man's nature, the image of the Divine stamped on mankind. No matter what riches are revealed in human nature, Man can never prove worthy of the adoration of men, and the questing mind must ultimately turn from it all in bewilderment to seek enlightenment from the Word of God. Through the Word of God, we learn that deep in our own nature God dwells, and that this is no mere metaphor for the reflection of the infinite things within us, but the expression of a literal truth. God, the Infinite, the Incomprehensible, has been pleased to create man in the image of His own infinity, and to take up His abode in the souls of men. By realizing this truth, we escape being enslaved by the finite things in our nature which would delude us with the pretence of our own Godless infinity, and we are lifted far above that only infinity which we can indeed claim—the infinity of our own weakness and limitations.

God is within us, not merely in the sense that by adopting us He sets us free from our own terrifying loneliness, though this in itself is a greater happiness than the world can give us. Knowing that we are dust in His sight, and humbly accepting the measureless distance between Him and us, we adore Him as more than just the Cause of our liberation. Without Him, we could not know ourselves as we really are. We raise our eyes to God and cry to Him, nothingness speaking to Eternal Being; and yet, we know with a rush of joy that He is the very source of our being, the meaning of our existence, and that, through grace, we are partakers in His Divine Life.

God is within us, as He has himself testified. We are "the temples of the Holy Ghost" and "the spirit of God" dwells within us as our true infinity. This spirit broods over us, filling us with the abundance of the plenitude of life, anointing us and sealing our hearts with a celestial seal. The earnest and first taste of life everlasting, He satisfies our insatiable craving for knowledge of what we are and what we mean. He is the Life in which our death is swallowed up. He is our unbounded happiness, through Whom we know a tearless joy even in the valley of tears. When we are weary and heavy in mind and heart, He is our secret source of consolation. We know that we often grope in the half-light of our own folly; and we find courage in the realisation that He is within us and that we can call on Him for guidance. We find the eternal love of God dwelling within us, even though our hearts are selfish and narrow; behind the dryness of our years we know there lives His eternal freshness; He is the sky of serene joy behind our heavy clouds of sorrow; in Him we find confidence to face the tasks from which we shudder; He is true liberty, through Whom our souls take wing towards eternal bliss.

To many, all this may seem the poetic weavings of mere wishful thinking, since we are not really aware that we have such treasure within us. This objection, however, is based on an outmoded idea; for the surface mind, thinking only in terms of materialistic being—that is to say, admitting the existence of consciousness alone—is an anachronism surviving from the "enlightenment" of the eighteenth and nineteenth centuries. Today, we know that the mind of man is not consciousness alone, and that below the level of consciousness are infinite possibilities, unfathomed depths, unmeasured horizons. We are far from having surveyed the range of our own nature. To use a homely comparison, we have as yet lived in a paltry gate-lodge, while in reality our heart is a stately mansion where dwell the hopes of all our happiness and where a glorious personal destiny awaits our shaping. It is a well-known fact, of course, that psychiatry has reached down into the depths of our nature and has stirred up much that may seem indeed slimy and repulsive, so that our soul might seem rather an abode of hate and lust and greed fit for a devil's habitation rather than for the temple of God. And yet, we must nourish our faith, in order that we may know the splendid message of joy in all this. The depths in us are not pools of stagnant bitterness, but the waters of infinity springing up into eternal life. It is easy to stir up the slime; but it needs faith to see, behind and through all these dark forces, a much more powerful force—the power of the presence of the Holy Ghost. We can conquer the depths of our own nature and thereby realize ourselves to the fullest, only by an adoring belief and acceptance of this Divine Presence. Thus we make ourselves *living* temples, through conscious acceptance of the Divine in the depths of our being. Only through such acceptance do we open our hearts and our lives to the full power of the Holy Ghost.

All this does not occur if we ourselves do not invite the Holy Ghost to speak live-giving words in our souls. He speaks within us in answer to the words He hears from us; and once we have heard His voice, the depths of our being are no longer a tangle of conflicting urges and shoreless immensities, but a window opening on real Infinity and a place alight with the fructifying presence of God. The bewildering infinities of human longings become swallowed up in His true and incomprehensible Infinity: in the mysterious designs of God, we become partakers, in our own finite way, of God's infinity. We cannot truly know ourselves except through this realization that our whole nature is in the image of God's immensity.

This brings us back to the subject of prayer. The Spirit of God dwelling within us as a great light in all our darkness, is the source of our prayer. He is not only God before Whom we kneel in supplication; He is working in us and for us, by His inspirations, especially when we are engaged in that most important of all our activities— prayer. In itself, our prayer consists of but dry words in arid minds; our pious feelings are in themselves but sickly plants languishing in the poor soil of our souls. But, through the power of the Holy Ghost within us, the words of our prayers become winged words, light-filled words, words that rise to the throne of God; and our pious feelings take deeper root, and blossom into spiritual strength and beauty. Thus, through our prayer, the Holy Spirit within us worships the Father and pleads for us "with unspeakable groanings"; and sometimes in our prayer we shall experience something of God's eternal joy in His own infinity and splendour. Herein is the secret of the great dignity of human prayer.

Since we are partakers in the Divine Nature, our prayer has a greater power than lies in mere human words. We pray, not only with what is human in us, but with what is divine. Mighty things, far beyond our understanding, occur within us when we say: "Our Father". They may seem to us to be drily spoken and to savour of presumption; but when sincerely spoken, the inner reality to which they correspond is something glorious. We are baptized children of God, professing our belief in Him and our love for Him; therefore the Spirit of God truly lives within us and speaks in us. Through the Holy Ghost dwelling within us, the words: "Our Father" are filled with a power of worship which links them with the praise of God by the Angelic choirs in Heaven.

We may not know for what we should ask when we pray; but it suffices that God knows. Our pleadings may seem to lose themselves unheard somewhere in the cold silent expanses that separate us from God; and yet, God not only hears us, but calls to us from His Immensity. In this faith, we cast out fear. Only God knows the depths of the human soul, and there is nothing hidden from Him. When He searches the depths in us, He does not find mere emptiness, aimlessness, the coiling and uncoiling of urges and passions, twisted and thwarted being; He sees His own Divine Spirit, and listens to the " unspeakable groanings " of that Spirit pleading in the prayer of the human soul. He hears those pleadings as His own pleadings in which the chaos of our hearts and of our lives is touched with Divine order and transformed into praise worthy of God.

The Holy Ghost is our help in prayer. When we are overcome with fatigue and spiritual dryness, so that the words we speak seem to fall heavy and lifeless about our feet, He prays within us with that freshness of praise we cannot command. When our lack of faith seems to wither the prayer on our very lips, He speaks words within us and for us which are not the image but the very substance of Divine Worship worshipping the Divine. Sometimes what we really think and feel seems to lag far behind the fervent words we speak in our prayer: we say—"My God, I love Thee"—and feel that the words are echoing only in our own hollowness. We then find courage and strength in the realization that the Holy Ghost dwelling within us is giving the true meaning to the words, speaking them with us in an adoring rapture of love. Always when we pray sincerely, from however dry a heart, the Spirit of God prays within us.

The Holy Ghost helps us, not only in our interior experience of prayer, but also by giving to our prayer a new and more exalted significance. Through Him, our prayer becomes one with the pure harmony of angelic prayer eternally rising like incense to the Blessed Trinity. The Spirit of God prays in us. This is the source of the confidence which enables us to pray. The Spirit of God prays in us. Herein is the sublime dignity of our prayer, and the inspiration urging us " always to pray and not to faint ". The unfailing power of our prayer is the Spirit of God praying within us. Because of this, our prayers are real, however arid the words on our lips and however dry our hearts. Because the Spirit of God prays within us, our prayer will become as a fountain springing up unto life everlasting.

Our prayer is made worthy of God through the Spirit of God. Before we begin to pray, let us silence the echoes from the commonplaces of life, that a deep interior silence may take possession of our souls. Only in that silence can the finer things within us be heard, and only when there is silence of the heart can grace work in us to inspire our prayer. Into that silence, the Spirit of the Father and of the Son will speak. Sometimes, through the actual grace of sensible devotion, we may be keenly aware of that voice in a rapture of joy; more often, we must believe in faith that He is speaking in us, with us and for us, that His words are being silently spoken in the depths of our being and in the Being of the Eternal Father. We must not do anything to hinder this speaking of the Holy Ghost through our prayer. We must speak His word: *Our Father,* with reverence and love. For this is true prayer.

III.

THE PRAYER OF LOVE.

OUR love of God and our prayer have one difficulty in common. They will succeed only if we lose the very thought of what we are doing in the thought of Him for Whom we are doing it. To be concerned mainly with the correct way to love or the correct way to pray, entails almost inevitable failure in the realization of either activity. It is useful to consider these matters in retrospect by meditating on the nature of the love of God and on the nature of prayer; it is useful to attempt to describe what the act of love or the activity of prayer really entails. Yet, to some extent, such meditation destroys the very act itself, for we cannot really perform an act and at the same time be preoccupied with the mechanics of our doing it. We succeed in prayer and in love only when we lose ourselves in both, and are no longer aware of *how* we are praying or in *what manner* we are loving. Our age is particularly given to introspection and the analysis of motive and action, with the result that we are often deprived of the power to act through sheer preoccupation with how the act is to be done. In the spiritual sphere, we become entangled in our own speculative thoughts about God and about the modes of our prayer, instead of entering into union with God through meditation and love. We lose our zest for the object of the activity in our zeal for the activity itself. Thus we become tangled with the very means to activity, and we cannot act. Our age is imprisoned in its own subjectivity. The modern tendency is to call on even the most exalted moments of the human mind to stand and unfold themselves, declare their identity, state what they are and how they ' work '; for the modern mind is fearful of mistaking the image and the symbol for the reality, of mistaking for pure spiritual currency what is in reality the cleverly deceptive coinage of baser cravings. All this creates a closed circle of sterile questioning in which men imprison themselves. Instead of leading men to reach out for the desired object, this kind of self-questioning leads only to further self-questioning and to a sterility in which there is no answer and no activity.

Today, we tend to judge our thoughts and feelings in themselves, and not by reference to the exalted nature of the object towards which they tend. This is a wrong attitude, because it leads to feelings of disillusionment in which our activities cease to have any real significance for us. Thus disillusioned, we are inclined to avoid altogether such acts as deliberate raising of mind and heart to God in prayer and love. God becomes for us the Ineffable, the Incomprehensible; and we live out our years in His sight dumb in mind and heart. He sees our good works on earth, our "little nameless unremembered acts of kindness" towards our neighbour, our fundamental decency, and the patience with which we bear the weight of "all this unintelligible world". We live, as it were, with our backs to God, knowing indeed that He is watching us, but never turning to speak to Him because we fear the very act of prayer. Hence the cult of a religion so prevalent today, which could be described as anonymous morality: *I don't pray and that sort of thing, but I am as decent a man as the next*, is the way this cult is usually worded. Those who still "pray and that sort of thing" are regarded as naïve, unanalytical, incapable of realizing that they are confusing God with their own thoughts and feelings *about* God. The proper attitude is, of course, to live decently and avoid the dangers of self-deception in all this praying and church-going. The Modern Mind has come to regard prayer and expression of one's love of God as at best redundant, and at worst mawkish and effeminate.

Let us examine more closely this fear of "direct" religion. On analysis, it is found to be an aspect of the modern fear of introspection: the fear of being caught up in a circle of subjectivity which sets off from the self and returns to the self, its only fruits being inner loneliness and a sense of futility. This fear freezes the springs of prayer, because prayer is regarded as something which inevitably leads *inwards* to the self, whereas the tendency is rather to reach *outwards* away from the self. Prayer is indeed such a "reaching out" to the Infinity of God, and has a significance far beyond the limitations of this earthly life. It is because modern man tends to suspect everything reaching beyond the narrow sweep of the five senses and of human reason, that he shrinks from the supernatural, except perhaps to the extent of passive belief. The great masters of the spiritual life have emphasised that the objective relationship existing between God and men demands a positive attitude in which men look up to God in faith, worship, hope and love, rather than adopt a remote, negative attitude in which they worship God indirectly through something other than God. All things lead to the direct worship of God Himself. Though Incomprehensible and above all His works, God can be known through His works. He has spoken to us in the Person of His Son, and it was in human words that the Son spoke to us of the Father. God has poured forth His Spirit into our hearts, but we know this only through the words of the Son. Therefore we may, and indeed we must, lift up our minds to God Himself, praise Him in our hearts, worship Him explicitly and publicly, honour Him, take courage to speak to Him and to call Him ' Father '.

All our activities take their meaning from Him. What our minds can know of Him, we love in Him, but mind and heart reach out to seize on the Unknown, the Incomprehensible, the Infinite. A thirst for the Infinite has been made part of the very essence of the human soul; and hence Saint Augustine's famous words: "Thou hast made us for Thyself, O Lord, and our heart is restless until it rests in Thee." While we remain on earth, we see things " through a glass, in a dark manner," as Saint Paul puts it, and the Spirit of God given to us remains a hidden God. That this is so, however, does not dispense us from the duty of Faith, for it is through Faith that our thirst for the Eternal finds its expression. Through Faith, man dares to reach away from himself towards a glory which as yet he can but glimpse, until that Faith is swallowed up in the Eternal Light wherein he meets his God face to face.

If God is regarded as the unknown factor which, being beyond the range of our practical life, can be ignored or at most accepted passively as one might accept the presence of an onlooker, then we can never experience a nearness to God, and our vague religion will pale, to all intents and purposes, into atheism. We must invoke the Mystery of God, ponder it, live with it, learn to love it; so that, even though it remains a mystery, it becomes a reality in our life.

Prayer is a lifting up of the heart, a directing of the mind, to God. In the language of Christian thought, love is that pure fulness of prayer in which man gathers up all his activities into a direct communication with God. The Commandment of Love is more than the fulfilment of the Law: it is also the essence of all true prayer. There is no need for specific formulae and set words in prayer, because in prayer we speak freely with God, offering our petitions, confessing our guilt, worshipping the infinite attributes of God. Men find themselves by yielding themselves entirely to God, and above all by giving to Him a love of which He alone is worthy—unconditionally, boundlessly, eternally worthy. Since the fulness of prayer is the love of God, it is through that love that we must learn what prayer really is.

What is the love of God, and how can we attain it so as to learn how to pray? We are told that this love shows itself in particular through the observance of the Commandments. This is indeed true; but it is not the whole truth. The love of God must precede and be the motive of such observance. Many efforts have been made to describe the love of God in the human soul. It is true, of course, that those who know how to talk about the love of God do not necessarily possess a greater measure of it. It remains nonetheless true, however, that when we hear others speak of the love of God, we come to realise how lacking we are in this love.

In speaking about the Divine Mysteries, even Holy Scripture had to fall back on thoughts and images drawn from human life. We may begin, therefore, from our human experience of human love. When one person loves another with a pure and unselfish love, that love gives some idea of the love we must bear to God, except that our love of God must be deeper, more unselfish, more unconditional, because it is directed towards God Himself.

The word *love* covers a variety of human relationships so that it is necessary to determine what one means by the term. The love we speak of here is certainly not the narrow and selfish idea of sexual lust. Even in cases where it does not degrade itself to promiscuity or excessive indulgence, sexuality falls short of the perfection of the ideal *love* in the context: *love of God*. On the other hand, the love of which we speak must not be confused with a feeling of benevolence which, even though it may prehaps be unselfish, is fundamentally supine. For this love is something essentially positive, passionate, arising from the very recesses of a man's soul, shattering his egotism, surging upward from the dust of its nothingness to its glory in the worshipping of the Infinite. Through such love, we lose ourselves in our union with One immeasurably greater than ourselves, Who has become the sole meaning of life for us.

Unselfishness is the essential quality of love, wherein the soul rejoices at the very existence of the beloved. It is a radiant release from the self, experienced when a man learns to break through the imprisoning walls of his own egotism and give himself to another. Beforehand, his life was a miserable one, cribbed and cabined: now it has taken on "an ampler ether, a diviner air" by escaping from its own self-shackles through giving itself to another. In complete forgetfulness of self, this love clings to the beloved. The happiness of the beloved is the happiness of him who loves. To love in this manner, is to have escaped from the prison of selfishness without being trapped into another prison. For this love of one person for another not only reveals the value of the beloved person, but opens up vistas of the mysterious and radiant wonders of the whole creation. In fact, this exchange of pure and unselfish love between two persons becomes the reflection and symbol of that Love which embraces all things—the Love of God.

But this love between two persons can lead to happiness or to misery. The secret of its happiness lies in the recognition by both parties, that through this love a greater love must be born. Their love for one another must meet in and be exalted by the greater Love. Again, the essence of human love is the realization that in giving oneself, one has received in return the gift of another. This gives a greater sense of security than when lived within oneself; for it is not good for a man to be alone. From the union of two loving hearts arise that thoughtful serving of one another and that unselfishness and fidelity which are at once the safeguards and the hallmarks of love.

Let us endeavour to love God in this fundamental way. Let us seek Him, the Almighty and Holy One, before Whom we are as dust. Forgetting ourselves, surrendering to Him our whole being, uniting ourselves to Him with every fibre of our souls, let us fling ourselves wide to God; and we shall know that bliss, at once yearning and sweet, which pervades us when we give to Him our whole being and our whole world. My Lord and my God! To Thee we may surrender ourselves entirely. Through Thee, what is hard in us becomes tender; and in our pure worship of Thee, we may reveal what we keep hidden from all. We can open our hearts freely to Thee, whispering to Thee what we are and what we do, our successes and our failures, our sorrows and our joys. In yielding ourselves entirely to Thee, we have no fear of being deceived. We lay our most precious treasures at Thy feet, and we know that our loving enthusiasm in doing so will not turn to the disillusion and bitterness of a betrayed love.

This love cries out to God in the depths of our hearts. All the powers of the soul well up to meet Him, and there is no ebb. God becomes the centre of our life, nearer to us than we are to ourselves, loved with a greater love than we bear to ourselves, loved unselfishly for His own sake. It is stained through with the inspired knowledge that it is He Who has first loved us. God never fails to answer the call of love rising to Him from the shadows of this valley of tears, because this love is utterly unselfish, faithful and gentle, seeking nothing but a return of love. It loves God rather than merely loving the reward which is promised to that love; for in the love itself, it is rewarded. Trials do not daunt it, nor is it quenched by the waters of sorrow. It is something quiet and hidden; at once bold and timorous; always marked with reverence for the Divine Mysteries, familiarity never breeding an absence of awe and wonder. It is not the love of a human person, but the love of God; and therefore the Infinite Greatness of the Object of love will be reflected in the reverence, humility and burning ardour of the lover. For the love of God is holy and sublime—and eternal.

This love is the true love of God, the Infinite One, Who dwells in our hearts in a mysterious manner that we cannot understand. It is the love of the Holy One, Who alone is worthy of adoration. We love Him with Whom we are to come face to face in life everlasting; Him Who is our Creator and our Lord; the Eternal Father, Son and Holy Ghost—three Divine Persons in one God. We love Him Who first loved us, Who gave us existence and life, in Whom we live and move and have our being, Who loves us even when we have turned our backs on Him. He is patient, faithful and wise; He is the God of our hearts and the God Who is our portion forever. Infinity lies between His Immensity and our nothingness, but this very Infinity is a challenge to our love inasmuch as it emphasises how much our whole life is dependent upon His adorable Providence. In awe and worship, we entrust our life into the hands of this beloved God. The more radiant His divine beauty and love, the more that love exceeds any conception we can have of love. By grace, the Divine becomes more living and real in us, so that thereby God becomes to us father and mother, brother and sister, our hearts growing more intimately united with His Divine Heart. Love is the soul's answer to the inscrutability of God's judgments and ways: the less able the soul finds itself to understand God, the more urgently its love reaches out towards Him. Overwhelmed by our utter nothingness in the face of God, we pray the more fervently: " My God, I love Thee "—words which are the highest expression of love that any man can offer. In the mystery of the love he bears towards an Infinite God, man realises what is most exalted in his nature.

But we must not misunderstand the nature of this love. True, it burns with the sacred fire of selflessness and self-oblation which is characteristic of all human love— be it only the fire where love turns to pain through its

37

own yearning. While this is so, however, the fire of the love of God has a higher nature, because its power is not *in itself* but derives from the fact that it is a flame of love rising to *God*. Hence it is that this love becomes true Christian love only when sanctified by Grace.

Several considerations flow from this. The love of God is indeed the highest exaltation of human nature; but it must be constantly preserved, through being continually sanctified, from degenerating into a mere expression of one's own presumptuous ability to become like unto God through one's own paltry resources. Nor should it become an expression of burning impatience to win God by our own efforts—to seize Him, as it were, by sheer power of will. The true love of God can exist only in a heart which is humbled by the unattainable majesty and unapproachable holiness of the Everlasting God. To be redeemed from ourselves, we must humble ourselves in adoration of the Almighty. We must control our thirst for that grace of sensible devotion which makes us experience the *nearness* of God : this must be left entirely in His hands, since what matters to us is only the doing of His holy will. The fire of our longing for God is pure only when it is kindled in us by the will of God. The love of God demands perseverance and self-restraint; and this is possible only by the grace of Him Who, dwelling eternally in the bosom of His Father, yet " emptied himself " to serve that Father in silent obedience in a sinful world.

The greatest and purest upsurge of human love falls short of that love which God wishes to receive from us. The divine paradox here is that we must love God with a love implanted in us by God; for this love, like everything we have received, and even like that Beatific Vision which we hope for in Everlasting Life, is a free gift of God, beyond our power to achieve or to merit by our own unaided efforts. Between us and God is the gulf between nothingness and Infinity. If our love reaches God across that abyss, it is solely because, through His Holy Spirit, God has cast into our hearts His own supreme Love, in which our sinfulness and our nothingness has been swallowed up. " God has first loved us " : Love has stooped to our nothingness and kindled itself in us. We were unworthy of this Love, and it is only through this Love that we can offer our love to God. For what is our love, but, as it were, a frightened surrender to that Divine Love that has been cast into our hearts as the fire which Christ said He had come " to cast upon the earth " with the desire that it " should be enkindled "? All our efforts to love would fail hopelessly, were they not mysteriously transformed, freely lifted to a higher plane above the reach of human effort, by Divine Love, through which we attain to that true love worthy of God and of redeemed creatures destined to enjoy the Beatific Vision. This true love of God becomes a living reality in us when we bear in mind that it is rooted in, and is the free gift of, God's love for us. Therefore our prayer of love must be: "Thou, O Lord, lovest me. Grant me the grace to open my heart to that love, that I may love Thee."

How are we to know that this love lives in us? The deepest things in a man are not those which abide his question most readily, nor about which he is most ready to speak. A love stronger than death can live unsuspected within a man. But our own honest opinion of ourselves is that we love God only in a half-hearted way —that, indeed, our love is often no more than a resolution and intention to love Him, far from that " with thy whole heart and with thy whole soul, with all thy mind and with all thy strength " which He Himself demands of us. Yet, we must love God more and more: otherwise, we shall have in the end to face the bitter realisation that our life has been useless because devoid of real love. We shall stand at the outer rim of our years like an errant child at the grave of a mother whose love for him he realizes too late to make a return of love.

It is said that we cannot command love—that we cannot *resolve* and *intend* to love—because the waters of love rise in obedience to their own mysterious laws. This is indeed true of merely human love. Yet, of one thing we can be certain. He who has honestly resolved to seek the love of God, may be said to possess that love already in his heart. For that very resolution is a proof that the grace of God has descended into the depths of his heart to kindle there a longing for God's love. What we must do is to set no obstacle to the growth of this love within us, so that it may pervade our whole being more and more. We must ask Him Who is the object of our love to give us the sweetly compelling power of His Grace; to reach into the depths of our soul, and set a spring of love there so that its waters may make fertile the dry and barren places of our lovelessness.

We often feel that our heart is stony, and that we have no power to warm it with love. There is, however, one thing we can all do: we can heed the first feeble stirrings of a love for God, the first timid longing of our restless hearts for God. The busy cares of life make us dusty and tired, so that even life's joys may become insipid. There are times when we feel cold and alone, our friends become as strangers to us, and even the love of our dearest fails to satisfy a deep longing in our innermost soul. Our world seems a meaningless tangle of empty hurryings to and fro, where the new turns out to be but the old wearing another face, where day follows pointless day, where knowledge arduously gathered lies cold and inert in the soul. Life ebbs, wealth becomes as sand running through one's fingers, friendship grows cold, the senses become blunted and without response. Such is every man's lot, but we do not regard such things as our real sufferings. For, in addition, there is all the bitterness that can fill the heart of a man—desolation, grief, distress and suffering both of body and of soul.

Grace comes when we are made to realise the futility and ephemeral nature of all things under the sun, and it is typical of human nature to resist this realisation. When one thing turns to dust and ashes for us, we turn from it hopefully to something else, and so the restless search goes on. This seed of restlessness placed in the human heart, though at first sight it may appear an unwholesome thing, is in reality a great blessing. For when a man has discovered that all his fevered searching leads only to blank walls of disillusion, he begins to experience a new realisation which makes a way for the love of God in his heart. There is only one object of love—God—that can fill the soul of man to its immortal girth—that can quench that thirst which drives a man restlessly on and on. God alone can possess us fully and satisfy us entirely. Hence, that disillusionment which makes the heart cry out its "vanity of vanities" over all earthly things, is essential to all Christians. It reveals to us that only One is capable of seizing upon our entire being, and that we must surrender to Him in unbounded love. Reeling under the impact of this disillusion, yet neither despairing nor blinding ourselves with any deception, we begin to grope towards the love of God which comes to us as "something else" about which we are as yet vague and uncertain, but which we know this world cannot give us. When, under the guidance of Grace, we recognize this vague yearning as a thirst for Infinity, for God, the love of God comes alive in our souls. Deeply implanted in human nature is a man's longing for the God of his heart and the God Who is his portion forever. All earthly things wither to disillusion, and of himself a man begins to seek God Who alone is Love. In Him alone does the heart find rest.

The way of quiet and grateful joy may also lead to our discovery of the love of God dwelling within us. Someone does us a great kindness, we are freed from a crippling fear or a heavy sorrow, and we feel a surge of deep joy and calm. Behind that change from sorrow to joy, from oppression of heart to freedom, we sense something greater. We read into this joy a reflection of eternal light, and in our gratitude, we know that we have met God and that He has blessed us. We are filled with a sense of His goodness, His greatness, His sublime mercy. We feel His nearness to us, and the luminous shadow of His blessing, awakening our love.

When we are thus visited by God through sorrow or through joy we must nourish the inward urge to love awakened in our souls. We must not turn from that timid longing for God that raises its small voice to speak to us of His love. It is a whispering voice which is quickly drowned if we do not shut out the clamouring noises of this world, the eager elbowing voices of business and pleasure. We must create in ourselves that interior silence in which we can subdue the restlessness of our heart, and breathe our silent prayer: " O God, near unto me, great and above all things, Thou alone art good. I love Thee."

In thus awakening the love of God within us, we have but begun. This first small stirring of love within us must survive in our day-to-day life. It must prove itself in faithful obedience and in love of our neighbour. It does not develop into firm and authentic love of God unless God transforms it, through the power of His Holy Spirit, into that love which alone can unite a man with God. Nevertheless, we must not underestimate the importance of these first feelings of sensible tenderness towards God, those first feeble steps of our own, wherein Grace comes to us amid the work of our own hands. For it is in this way that the true love of God is born within our heart.

This mysterious rising of the waters of love within the hidden depths of our soul, this longing for God which requires only our willing consent, could well up with greater power if we had not choked its source with the dust of our sins. We experience in practice the truth of Christ's words: " Blessed are the clean of heart, for they shall see God." Only a person whose heart is pure, or who has at least a sincere and active desire for this purity of heart, can truly love God, the Source of all goodness and all purity. Repeated grievous sins extinguish the love of God in the soul; and venial sin and bad habits impede its growth. We observe the strict duties of the Christian life, perhaps, but we regard as unnecessary and supererogatory anything beyond what is strictly prescribed. Our conscience is easily satisfied, and we have no real anxiety about our salvation. We show a reluctance to prayer and the reception of the Sacraments, and our spiritual obligations are things to be got through as expediently as possible so as to get back to what we regard as the more pleasant things in life. Now, all this prevents us from loving God with our whole heart. We stand before God as persons who are spiritually blind and dumb.

The soul that loves God welcomes the sense of God's love in the performance of every duty, thereby transforming each duty into an act of love. The sin-ridden self-centred soul, however, fears that God may demand that which it is unwilling to give, and is therefore reluctant to meet God. We must obey the promptings of our conscience, by earnestly and perseveringly doing our duty in every moment of our life. By doing so, we bring God into our daily life, and we draw nearer to Him. We grow in the knowledge of His holiness and His goodness, and thus cultivate that purity of heart through which the soul becomes united with God. In this way, we begin to love God with our whole heart and our whole soul, with our whole mind and our whole strength.

We must foster the first stirring of our heart, and we must keep our heart pure in readiness for the love of God. Above all, however, we must pray for the gift of divine love and for that purity which is essential to its presence. It is in the hands of God to control the beginning, the growth and the perfection of sacred love in us, according to His own Divine Will; for He has first loved us. The first stirring of sacred love within us was the effect of His grace. He, and He alone, can purify our hearts. We must pray for this grace, and for an increase of His love. We may well fear that our hearts will become cold to God's love, and may wonder whether indeed we do not love darkness more than we love light. All the more reason, therefore, to implore His compassionate mercy to give us ever increasing spiritual strength, so that His love may grow in our hearts.

O Jesus, give us a fear and love of Thy Holy Name, for Thou art ever present to guide and preserve those whom Thou hast established firmly in Thy love.

The love of God is the greatest grace which can be given to mankind. In it, human life achieves its true fulness, for in it we find happiness, an end to the restless searchings of our heart, and the very essence of Everlasting Life. No prayer is more certain to be heard than the petition that God may take us to His Heart, and that we may desire only the riches of His love.

Let us therefore pray: " Make me love Thee, by God, Neither in Heaven nor on earth have I anything but Thee, O God of my heart and my Portion forever. Make me cling to Thee. O beloved Lord, be Thou the centre of my heart: purify it that it may truly love Thee. Thy holiness, Thy beauty, Thy goodness are my happiness. Stay with me when I am tempted to leave Thee. Do not forsake me: make Thy love grow in me, for that love is eternal, and without Thee I am nothing. Through this love, I fervently hope to be united with Thee in Life Everlasting."

IV.

PRAYER IN EVERYDAY LIFE.

PRAYER is a voice from the depths of the heart, and there is nothing more sublime on earth than a pure heart filled with faith and charity. Prayer is the language in which the heart asks God to hear it, and to take it lovingly to His own heart. There is nothing more moving or more sublime that this loving attention on the part of the Eternal Father to the feeble stammering of His child. True prayer is prayer in the Holy Spirit. There is nothing more awe-inspiring or more sublime that this voice of the Spirit, at which all eternity trembles. The abyss between man and God is bridged when, on the wings of prayer, the feeble words of the creature are carried to the throne of the Creator. The voice of human supplication reaches to the heights wherein dwells the Majesty of God in eternal bliss. He who has truly understood what a sublime thing prayer is, must be stricken with awe indeed when he is about to pray.

How then can prayer be an everyday business, compatible with the monotony, uniformity, depression and dullness of our hearts, so tired and desiccated? Yet there must be something like prayer in everyday life, for the Scripture says that we ought " always to pray and not to faint." (Luke 18:1). St. Paul admonishes us to " pray at all times in the spirit " (Eph. 6:18), to " pray without ceasing " (I. Thess. 5:18) and to be " instant in prayer " (Rom. 12:12).

Let us consider two aspects of everyday prayer. We are to pray in everyday life, and we are to make everyday life our prayer.

We are to pray in everyday life. This should be regular prayer, practised without regard to our humours or likings. We mean here that prayer which, without being specifically enjoined, is practised from an innate sense of duty or as a cherished tradition—prayer at certain times, such as when retiring and before meals. Prayer in everyday life includes the Angelus, the Rosary said by the individual or by the family, and visits to the Blessed Sacrament outside the times of public service. Prayer in everyday life includes many pious customs we have inherited from our forefathers, such as our salutation when we pass a church or a Crucifix, the sign of the cross when we cut a new loaf of bread, the blessing received at night by children from their parents. All these things are essentially prayer in everyday life.

Such prayers have their own difficulties. Many of us find it hard even to remember them. In many Catholic countries they have fallen into disuse or oblivion. Those of us who still are Christians know that we are bound to such prayer at least by custom: yet in many places these customs have a precarious existence, since minds and hearts are filled with other things. We are told that modern man has no time for such prayers. They appear old-fashioned. They have become mere memories of childhood days. Never officially abolished, they drag on a miserable life without exercising any formative influence. We are inclined to think that, by dropping these relics of childhood, nothing would really be changed, for better or worse.

Prayer in everyday life is difficult. It is easily forgotten, since our rushed and fevered age does not foster and promote it. It thrives only in individual hearts, which, unconcerned with the disbelief of others, can instil their own vigour into everyday prayer from their own lively and personal faith.

It is difficult to prevent everyday prayer from disappearing imperceptibly and withering away. It is even more difficult to make everyday prayer *real* prayer and to prevent its degenerating into mere routine. We must ask ourselves how far our everyday prayer is more than mere words. Heart and mind are often far away from what we are saying. Instead of speaking heart to heart to God, we recite set formulas. Our main concern is to get through the formulas, and there is no attempt to establish vital contact with God. Thus everyday prayer becomes an everyday matter in the worst sense of the word. It becomes a superficial, mechanical, slipshod lip-service, the performance of an external task to be got through as quickly as possible in order to get back to more pleasant things.

Such prayer is, as it were, time grudgingly conceded to God, because this concession is better not omitted, lest we should get into His bad books. Thus we slip into that terrifying state of everyday Christian life, where in praying, our hearts remain far from God. Our lips honour God, but our heart does not join with them; and yet we imagine that we thus fulfil our duty towards God. Towards Him Who alone knows our heart, however, there is no fulfilment of duty unless our life and words are filled with the pure spiritual intention of the heart.

In many cases, a man suffers because of the difference between what his prayer is and what he knows it should be. He suffers from his heart's refusing to enter into the lofty words of adoration, praise, thanks, petition, awe or contrition, which are the subject and expression of prayer. He suffers from the contrast between his willingness to pray, often and every day, and his apparent incapability. His heart seems to be paralysed, and he fears he may be labelled a hypocrite through pretending to do something which in reality is beyond his power. He thinks that in sincerity towards himself and towards God, he must wait until the fountains in the depths of his heart spring up again, to provide the healing waters of grace, of spontaneous emotion and of vital spiritual experience, thus making true prayer possible in a sincere outpouring of the heart. This difficulty tempts many a responsible and good person to pray infrequently. These are persons whose everyday life becomes void of prayer, not because they have succumbed to the superficiality of mundane routine, but because they are conscientious and honest. They refuse to pray unless their prayer comes from the heart. They do not believe that it needs only the will of man to make his prayer the voice of the heart.

Nevertheless, in spite of all these difficulties, it remains true, as the wisdom of our forefathers and our own precious inheritance teach us, that we must make prayer part of our daily life. We must not restrict prayer to the rare moments of sensible devotion when prayer wells up spontaneously within us. Such moments do indeed occur as long as faith in God lives in the soul. We must realise the necessity of everyday prayer, which is both the prerequisite and the result of those great moments of spiritual exaltation.

There are, of course, considerable differences in the quality of various moments of prayer. There are certainly prayers, perhaps in but fleeting and rare moments, when an Angel of God touches our heart, and when our heart is filled with awe at the majesty of the real presence of God. In those moments we experience a veritable nostalgia for our eternal home. In those moments we are inspired by the hope of the peace of God, in contrition transforming our life, in love of the eternal Love. These moments must certainly be treasured more highly than the prayer of everyday life. We may indeed be inclined to confine the name of prayer to those rare moments.

Yet those moments of grace are indeed rare. What would they profit us if they did not really capture our whole life and lift it on their wings. How spiritually impoverished we would become if in the course of our life they became imperceptibly more rare and less urgent, like inspiration in the brain of a dilatory artist? Such danger of spiritual desiccation cannot be overcome except through daily prayer. Only by our daily prayer can we create the prerequisite for the great moments of real prayer. Only when we make the effort, however hard it may be, to keep our heart open, our mind awake, and our attention alert, can we be in readiness to avail of these great and rare moments of grace. In those moments, God will suddenly meet us anew, and we shall receive an impetus which will inspire us for some time to come. We must not miss that impetus. We must always be prepared for it. In an hour of trial, of temptation, of ecstatic joy or crushing sorrow, in an hour of unspeakable loneliness or abysmal suffering, we may be called upon to give an answer which can be rendered only in prayer, an answer decisive for time and eternity.

This openness of the heart, this alertness of the mind, this constant preparedness for the great hour, will not be ours unless we have followed the command of the Lord: " Watch and pray." We must then draw on the resources we have accumulated through everyday prayer. Not to pray daily means that we are ignoring God, not listening for His word, and not preparing every day for our decisive trials. Thus we are in danger of becoming gradually blind and deaf, indifferent and lazy. In fact, we will even become unable to notice the decisive moments when we are at the cross-roads of life. A sudden storm will find us without foundation. We will lose our bearings in any new or unexpected situation, unless we have accustomed ourselves to watching in prayer day by day. We will not stand our ground in that decisive hour when life and death are in the balance, because it will arrive imperceptibly without warning, and we will not be able to plead that we have been taken by surprise. We will not be permitted to say we did not foresee the consequences, when we have refused to keep alert, active and watchful through daily prayer. Important matters, both intellectual and spiritual, are decided by the degree of practice we have acquired at the moment of discharging them.

When the hour of God, of sensible devotion in prayer has passed, we must prevent it from becoming a mere fruitless memory. It must be continued, by patient cultivation, into our ordinary daily life. The routine of everyday life must be enlivened and transformed by that vision granted to us for a brief moment in charismatic prayer. This decisive transformation cannot take place except through everyday prayer. Under the burden and amid the toil of everyday life, we must wrestle with God's angel of grace. That grey Monday morning and that weary Saturday night must yet be transfigured to some extent by a reflection of eternal light. The fire of the spirit that descended upon us in an hour of fervour, must cast its transforming reflection over the hours of daily life. We must pray for the descent of this fire upon us, as earnestly as we can. Only in virtue of such prayer will the spirit of that fire really permeate our life, which after all is mostly woven of small grey moments. Everyday prayer is both the prerequisite and the fruitful expansion of the great hours of grace in the Christian life. For that reason alone, it is important and essential.

A further, even more important, reason for prayer in everyday life is the honour of God. God is the Lord not only of the holydays of life. He has created not only sublime things: it is His holy will that the little things also should live and that He should be glorified in what appear to us the insignificant monotonies of our life. We are His servants not only in lofty cathedrals where His mysteries appear to us in overawing splendour and enrapturing beauty. We are His servants also in the field or the workshop, at the desk or at the washtub. All this is for the honour and glory of His Name. Therefore in this everyday life we must bear in mind that we belong to Him in every department of our lives. Through our whole life, His praise must rise up to heaven, and everything must be done in His Name. Again and again, we must utter the words that invoke His blessing upon our daily life. Hence we must be careful to pray daily.

Prayer in daily life may appear to us to be something as dreary as our daily life itself. It may have little room for lofty thoughts and sublime feelings. It is not a grand oratorio in a cathedral, but just a pious folksong, full of good intentions and straight from the heart, even if somewhat monotonous and simple. Prayer in everyday life is a prayer of fidelity and reliability. It is a prayer of unselfish, even apparently unrewarded service of God. It is the consecration by which the grey hours become bright and the little moments great. Such prayer does not seek a vital human experience, but only the glory of God. It is not a quest for experience, but for an increase of faith. It may sometimes seem very pedestrian: yet it carries us spiritually forward. Sometimes it seems to come merely from the lips, but it is better that at least the lips should continue to give praise to God rather than that a man should become silent altogether. When the lips speak, though the heart is silent, there is still hope that one day the heart will speak also. What in periods of spiritual aridity is described as mere lip-service in prayer, is in reality the prayer of a poor, yet faithful heart. Despite weakness, depression and weariness, a small shaft is again and again dug by honest labour, and through that shaft a ray of eternal light falls upon a heart buried by the débris of daily life.

We must pray in everyday life. Again and again, weariness and indifference must be overcome. We must endeavour to make our prayer a matter of our heart. We must make our daily prayer a deliberate attempt to turn our minds from busy concern with our mundane affairs, that we may be able to commune in a vital manner with God in the silence of our hearts. This cannot be done as long as we simply cling to a few set formulas which we have probably learnt as children.

We must pray regularly. We must strive to discharge in a *living* way and in *living* words, what we regard as our duty to pray. We must master our moods and feelings; and we can do so only by praying regularly.

It is only by grace that we can learn how to pray, but our willingness to pray and our perseverance in praying play an important part. We must learn to concentrate, in interior silence, on what we are about to do, namely to lift up our hearts. We must learn to speak to God without using set words; we must speak to Him of our necessities, of our daily life, in particular of that secret resistance against speaking to Him about our duties. We must speak to Him of our loved ones, of our moods, of the world and its needs, of the dead who have gone before us, and of Himself. Our words must tell of His greatness and distance, incomprehensible and yet wonderful, of His truth in contrast to our untruth, of His love and our selfishness. He is Life, while we are death; He is fulfilment while we are but longing. We must also learn to mute those things which keep us anxious and tensed, if we wish to attain to real interior quietude. The voice of our soul must become audible to us, that soul which is shy and uses so few, though such essential, words. Prayer is a song that can be sung only to God in the stillness of our hearts.

We must learn to make the reading of Holy Scripture really prayerful. Our evening prayer should give the scattered experiences of the day a unified meaning by directing them towards God. Rounded off with prayer, the day will enter into those deep recesses of the soul where the past is preserved without hatred or bitterness, in kindness and calm, in contrition without fear, in earnest dedication to God. We must learn to sanctify by prayer the dead moments in our daily life when we seem to have nothing to do, when we must wait or queue. The small annoyances and joys of the day can become reminders to us of God and of prayer. All these things can be learnt and practised. Make it your business to learn these things. Make it your habit to pray in everyday life.

Make everyday life your prayer. Happy is he who in his daily life returns again and again to prayer. Moreover, there is a higher aim to be achieved in the consecration of everyday life by prayer. Those who return again and again to prayer will never be completely overcome by everyday life; but the suffering of one's spiritual life from the cares of the world is not yet quite conquered. Even though we frequently pray in our daily life, this life itself seems to remain what it always was—a consistent, grey monotony. Our soul seems to continue its weary way on the road followed endlessly by the multitude with its innumerable trifles, its gossip and pretence, its curiosity and vanity. Our soul seems to remain in the marketplace where, from all quarters, the hawkers congregate to sell the petty goods of the world, and where in stultifying restlessness men, including ourselves, wander about offering their trifles. Our soul in daily life seems to be in a gigantic barn into which cartload after cart-load is brought, day by day, until it is filled to overflowing with mundane things. There is no end in sight. One day after the other, we go on in this way to the hour of our death, when all the goods and chattels which we called our life, will be swept away.

What will we be then and what will remain of us, whose life was nothing but the business of the day, idle talk and vain pretence? What will be the outcome of our life when at the last judgment the true essence of our hollow life and of the many days and long years that have remained empty, will be relentlessly revealed? Will anything remain beyond those few moments in which the grace of love or of an honest prayer to God shyly found a corner of our life otherwise filled with ephemeral rubbish?

It is of supreme importance to escape from this empty routine. Through the humdrum of our daily life we must find our way to Him Who alone is necessary, to Him Who alone is the Lord. Our everyday life must become a hymn of praise, indeed it must become in itself prayer. It is obvious that we cannot pray directly all the time. We cannot escape from daily routine, because it will go with us wherever we go. Everyday life is our life, and our everyday heart, our weary mind and our meagre love which abases all that is great, will ever remain with us. Thus we have to keep to the highway of our everyday life, its cares and duties. Nor must this routine be purely of intention. God must be sought and found in the things of our world. By regarding our daily duties as something performed for the honour and glory of God, we can convert what was hitherto soul-killing monotony, to a living worship of God in all our actions. Everyday life must become itself our prayer.

But it can become prayer only through unselfishness and love. If we are willing and understanding disciples, we cannot find a better means of growing in spirituality than through our everyday life. There are the long monotonous hours of work, for which often no recognition is given, the continuous and painful struggle which receives little reward, the weariness and the sacrifices of old age, disappointment and failure, adversity and misunderstanding. There are the many wishes denied to us, the many small humiliations, the almost inevitable opinionatedness of old age and the equally frequent inconsiderateness of youth. There are such things as physical discomfort, the inclemency of the elements, the friction of human contacts. Through these and a thousand other trials in which everyday life abounds, a man can learn to become calm and unselfish, if he only understands these task-masters, mundane and yet providential. He must willingly accept them, rather than try to ward them off. Such vicissitudes must be borne without complaint, as a matter of course. They must be accepted as incidental to the normal course of life.

In this way, we can use everyday life to fight our selfishness, slowly but certainly, since the guidance showered upon us by God in daily life is always certain and sure. In this way, the love of God will grow of itself in our hearts, a love both calm and chaste. It is men themselves who prevent the growth of this love. In everyday life we can mortify ourselves without vanity and without ostentation. Nobody will notice our efforts, and we ourselves will be scarcely aware of our mortification; yet, through the myriad occupations of our daily life, one defence after another will be thrown down, behind each of which our selfishness had entrenched itself. At last, when we have ceased to put up new defences, when we have learnt to accept our precarious human situation and rely on the grace of God, we will notice suddenly and almost cheerfully, that those defences were quite unnecessary. We will realise that it need not mean misfortune, if life deprives us of this or that joy hitherto regarded as indispensible. We need not despair when we fail or when our plans do not work out. Through everyday life, we are taught that we become rich in giving, that we advance spiritually through holy resignation, that we are blessed in sacrifice and that we find love when we give love to others. Thus a man becomes unselfish and free. This freedom makes us worthy of the supreme love of the ever free and infinite God, Who first loved us.

It is of supreme importance that we should achieve this conquest of our everyday life, because otherwise we allow ourselves to be dragged down to its level. Nothing can free us so much as this conquest. If we succeed, the love thus engendered will suffuse all the things of this world with the infinity of God, through a holy desire to exalt all the humdrum activities of daily life unto a hymn of praise to the glory of God. The cross of everyday life is the only means by which our selfishness can die, because in order to be utterly destroyed our selfishness must be ceaselessly crucified. This fruit of that cross will be a love born from the death of our selfishness. Thus, through love, fidelity, faith, preparedness and surrender to God, our everyday actions are tranformed into lived prayer.

Our life remains what it was, difficult, monotonous and unspectacular. It must remain what it is, for only in this way can it serve the love of God. Only in this way will it redeem us from ourselves. Through the sanctification of our everyday life, our desires, our reluctances, our stubbornness and our assertiveness, must be purified. Bitterness must cease to taste bitter. Routine must lose it monotony. Disappointment must cease to be sterile. Everyday life must train us to kindness, patience, peacefulness and understanding; to meekness and gentleness; to forbearance and endurance. In this way, everyday life becomes in itself *prayer*. All our interests are unified and exalted by the love of God; our scattered aims are given a specific direction towards God; our external life becomes the expression of our love of God. Thus, our life takes on a new meaning in the light of our Eternal Destiny.

Make everyday life your prayer. Pray for this great art of Christian living, as difficult to master as it is essentially simple in itself. Pray in everyday life, and so make everyday life your prayer. The sorrowful and fleeting days of our life, passed in monotony and banality, in commonplace pursuits and in toil, will merge with the Day of God, the great Day that has no evening. Let us pray daily for the coming of that Day, so that in us the words of St. Paul may be fulfilled: "I am confident of this very thing, that He Who hast begun the good work in you, will perfect it unto the day of Christ Jesus" (Phil. 1 : 6).

V.

PRAYER IN OUR NEEDS.

OF all types of prayer, the one which is most often arraigned before the bar of human judgment is the prayer of petition. " I have prayed," cries the anguished, embittered human voice from the wilderness of its pain, " and God has been deaf to my pleadings." In human affairs, accusations and denunciations may be justified in certain cases; and we must remember that however clearly the innocence of the accused may be established, the very necessity for such defence is regarded as in some sense a tacit admission of guilt. From this point of view, it becomes immediately evident how difficult it is to defend the worth of the prayer of petition against those who denounce it as vain and useless. We must listen seriously and with great human sympathy to such denunciations, for they came from those on whom the burden of life has pressed most heavily and who think that God has failed them. Despite all this, however, we must renew our faith in such prayer, and uphold its vital necessity.

Life itself is the accused, and embittered hearts are the self-appointed judges. The witnesses for the prosecution are the great weary mass of those whose lives are shadowed with unhappiness, misery and pain. Their name is legion; for a vivid sense of one's own unhappiness is fostered in nearly all of us by brooding and self-pity. We may sift the evidence for the prosecution, and dismiss from the case those witnesses who are motivated by sheer insolence and petty grumbling, as well as those whose grounds for complaint are frivolous and unworthy of notice. Yet, when all this has been done, the poverty and misfortune of the vast majority of mankind qualify them to enter the witness stand in the case against the worth of prayers of petition. These witnesses come from everywhere, from all nations, age-groups and social classes; and they all voice the same denunciation, born of despair or disappointment, of incensed or weary scepticism about the prayer of petition. It is a monotonous cry that goes on and on.

" We have prayed," sobs the weary chorus, " but God has not answered. We have cried, but there has been no response. Our cheeks have been wet with burning tears, but in vain. Too well indeed could we have proved to Him that our little requests demanded no great concessions from Him Who is Almighty. Nay more, we could have shown how the granting of our requests would have been but the manifestation of His glory on earth, the furthering of His Kingdom among men. We could even have held out the cold threat that His lack of response was the annihilation of our belief in Him as a Father of mercy and compassion—or indeed our belief in His very existence. And we are justified in being embittered by His silence. File after file we lay before Him: the unheard prayers of children dying from starvation and of infants frozen by paralysis; the cries of children beaten to death, of exploited slaves and betrayed women, of those crushed by injustice, liquidated in concentration camps, mutilated and dishonoured. Only the silence of God meets those bewildered questions raised to heaven by perplexed minds in every age: Why do the wicked prosper, and the good fail? Why does the lightning strike both the good and the wicked? Why must children suffer for the sins of their parents? Why can truth be abused in such a brazen fashion? Why is world history a swirl of stupidity, meanness and brutality?

" We could continue by appealing to His honour and His glory, and above all to His Name Which He wills should be honoured among men. He must take care that his guiding Hand can be clearly seen in the world of men; otherwise, this world becomes a meaningless chaos wherein there is no evidence of His wisdom, His justice and his goodness. Surely this demands that His help should come to us so clearly marked as Divine that our enemies cannot dismiss it as due to natural causes and therefore proving nothing. May we not demand a greater warrant of success from God than that given us by the laws of chance? Otherwise, life becomes a mere lottery, and it makes no difference whether we pray before or after a purely accidental stroke of luck. It would be quite unscientific to ascribe to God what is simply the outcome of mere chance.

" We could have spoken to God of His Son, Who knows how we think and feel, since He has shared our human life. All this we could have done—and, indeed, all this we have done. Did we pray? Of course we did. Did we follow His own counsel, by subjecting the King-dom of Heaven to the " violence " of our impetration? Our eager words have burst into flame before the very throne of God—and all in vain. We have cried like lost children seeking the kind and guiding hand, but no one came to wipe away our tears and speak words of comfort. We have prayed, but we have not been heard. We have cried to God, but He did not answer. We were speaking only into a gulf of silence. Indeed, our pleadings were saved from becoming ridiculous and absurd merely by the fact that they were voices from the depths of suffering and despair."

The case for the prosecution is complete: the accusa-tions against the prayer of petition have been pleaded from every angle. But what is the verdict of the jury? There is a division into a convinced majority and an equally convinced minority, both sections, however, reaching the conclusion by different roads that prayer is useless against human misery. For the majority, there is no God Who hears our petitions. Either He does not exist at all, or He dwells in a remote glory far beyond the reach of our prayers. He allows His creation to work His glory, through its blood and its pain. His calm un-concern is like that of the gods " careless of mankind," who, as the poet says,

> "smile in secret, looking over wasted lands,
> Blight and famine, plague and earthquake, roaring
> deeps and fiery sands,
> Clanging fights, and flaming towns, and sinking ships,
> *and praying hands*."

In moments of respite from pain, mankind may even in-dulge in some philosophising about the remoteness of God. Why should God stoop to an undignified meddling with the petty affairs of a petty world He has Himself created? At the outset, He must have set this clockwork world spinning with the utmost accuracy, to last as long as He willed. He must be now unaware even of its humming. The world was designed by Him to have its own complete meaning; it was not intended that He should perpetually stoop to it, to adjust and rearrange what He had already created adequate in itself. It is childish, therefore, to address petitions to God, for they are an insult to the omnipotence of God and a presumptuous overrating of our own importance. This is the line of reasoning taken by a person whose life is, for the moment, reasonably comfortable. Our salaries, our doctors, our police have their uses; but there is no need for the prayer of petition. But let things take a turn for the worse, and this same person is vehemently protesting that the prayer of petition is useless, because God has not rushed to anticipate his petition even before he had voiced it. Thus the mentality of the majority of the jury.

The minority hold a different opinion. They indeed tolerate prayers of petition, but only when such petition concerns the lofty needs of the soul. Our prayer to God must not degrade itself by becoming a concern for our daily bread, for bodily health, for long life, for protection from lightning and from catastrophes; nor should we pray to be shielded from pestilence, famine or other tribulations. We must pray only for purity of heart, for patience, for willingness to endure such sufferings as God may will to send us. Our prayers of petition are regarded as childish when they concern such protection and shielding from suffering, since they imply a lack of readiness to accept unconditionally the designs of God towards us. Rather than seek to have sufferings deflected from us, we should ask God for strength to bear the crosses He wills to send us. Apart from a few alleged miracles in answer to prayer—miracles of doubtful authenticity—the benefits reaped from the prayer of petition are of a spiritual kind, for this is the only type of largesse dispensed by God. The world pursues its inexorable course, the law of cause and effect functions ruthlessly in every age, and it is in vain that we hope to alter this by our tears or by our prayers.

Thus, then, the majority verdict and the minority verdict. According to the first, we are coldly alone on this earth, and cannot hope for any heavenly assistance; according to the second, we may indeed look to heaven for spiritual strength, but it is presumptuous of us to seek protection and material aid, since God does not listen to such pleas.

It is against God that this manifold indictment is drawn up. But He has preserved unbroken silence through age after age. Through His messengers, He has told mankind that He will not speak until the Day of Judgment; and meantime the accusations will pile up continually—accusations wrung from sorrow, accusations from those who "search into high matters", accusations on the lips of the cynical, accusations from those whose hearts lead their heads, accusations which reveal a spirit of infidelity.

Yet, despite this urgent plea against it, we feel a deep need to turn to God and lift pleading hands of prayer to Him. All these accusations are a source of distress to us, because we cherish a profound faith which cannot be shaken, despite what seem endless disappointments. We have been told: "When ye pray, ye shall say: Our Father . . . give us this day our daily bread." We have no wish to argue with God, to convince Him that our will is His glory; we are content to call humbly upon His mercy. Nor have we any desire to search into the secrets of life, to anatomise prayer, to question its *why* and its *wherefore*; we simply want to learn how to pray. It is not our aim to meet this case for the prosecution with a defence shattering in its greater logic and cogency. Suffice that we know we are suspended over the abyss of our nothingness by a thread of the mercy of God, and that we cling to that mercy. We seek only such light and strength as will enable us to persevere in prayer, lest our courage should fail us and our prayer turn to ashes in our mouth. We desire only the strength to persevere in the face of disappointment, while we await that Day wherein will be justified "the ways of God to men." In that Day, we shall be comforted and we shall understand all.

However, when we set aside for a moment our obsessive preoccupation with the pursuit of happiness on earth—which, after all, is not our purpose in life—we can listen to divine promptings which suggest a number of answers to those who would dismiss the prayer of petition as vain and useless. Why, our conscience whispers, do we suddenly demand God's assistance in disasters brought on us by our own sins? We cry out only when such disaster hits *us*, whereas we were perfectly contented and unmoved in face of the misfortunes of others. There is a certain hypocrisy in our attitude: while we thought we could get along quite nicely on our own, we ignored God; and now, when we find things getting too much for us, we call upon Him. He had no part in us when life smiled on us. But now our little nest of content is shaken by rough winds, and we expect the Kingdom of Heaven, so blissfully ignored, to be immediately concerned with setting things right again for us, in order that we may again be in the " happy " state of having no need of God. We have never really grasped that the glory of God in this world is the Cross of His Son.

We profess our belief in the everlasting happiness of heaven, but we want from this life as much comfort as is demanded by those whose thoughts do not reach beyond it. With a worldly shrewdness which is the very negation of the Christian spirit, we want our " bird in the hand " as well as our " birds in the bush "—happiness here as well as hereafter—in fact, the best of both worlds. We complacently regard our successes as the well-earned blessing and approval given by God to our work; and when He fails thus to bless with success our self-centred undertakings, we sternly ask what we have done to deserve such treatment. Childishly impatient, we are incapable of waiting for that Day wherein God will end His long silence by calling to the Great Reckoning the teeming generations of mankind. He has Eternity wherein to set right what appears to have gone astray in the course of Time. Do we really understand who God is, and who we are? Do we realise that, since He is the omniscient God, His ways and His judgments are beyond our powers of understanding? Do we understand that a creature cannot claim to be judge of the Creator? "Whom the Lord loveth, He chastiseth " seems blatant paradox to worldly wisdom, which cannot understand that the ways of God are so inscrutable that even His love and mercy must needs appear to us to be wrath and vengeance.

Let us repeat: all our suffering stems from our sins. We have refused to relinquish the cause, and now demand that God should deliver us from its effects, but leave us the cause. Which of us can honestly claim that he has not deserved this or that suffering? We are all sinners, and therefore we deserve greater suffering than any we are called upon to endure. Of course, a thousand excuses for sin are ready to hand: heredity, the pull of circumstances, the absence of the real malice of a desire to rebel against God. Surely God must understand that we are weak, that we want a bit of happiness in a grim world, that the fruit of the forbidden tree is sweet to the senses, that the tree of goodness has a somewhat ascetic taste. Besides, the fruit of that forbidden tree hangs down temptingly, while one is forced to reach up painfully for the fruit of the tree of good. Yes, surely God must make allowances.

Such are the sophistries with which we try to evade our guilt. Yet, sin is a crime against the Most Holy, and sin is our doing. Why do we not endeavour to minimise our sufferings by similar sophistries? In our own time, we have heard the theory propounded that it is good for the race that a certain section of mankind should go under periodically in the struggle for survival. Most of us have listened unmoved to eugenic theories and theories about racial purity, about the elimination of the "inferior" stock. On what grounds should we complain, if we happen to belong to a group marked for elimination? If the honour of God and the will of God are regarded as so unimportant, by what criterion do we set a value on our own wishes? God says to us " When you are angry and embittered, do not forget who *you* are and Who *I* am." Why, indeed, should we complain because God does not give to our prayers the answer demanded by our persistent selfishness?

It is not God Who must prove to us that He is good and holy: it is we who are called upon to show that we do not need the bait of constant reward to keep us faithful in our love. Sometimes the clouds gather and all seems impenetrably dark. It is then that we are called upon to love in faith—to nurse our firm belief in the stars of sweet reasonableness that continue to shine behind the darkness of events which seem to us sour and grim and beyond our understanding. That our limited sense-bound minds cannot fathom the ways of God, does not mean that He no longer exists. "O man, who are thou that repliest against God" (Rom. 9:20).

Let us now consider the evils from which we pray to be delivered. Are we so sure that, measured by the standards of God, they are really evils? They may indeed be so, and therefore God would have us ask Him to deliver us from them. But it is for Him to judge, and we must not anticipate His decision. We must realise how often the true meaning of our petition is: "Give us abundance, health, security and peace, and *then* we will love and serve you sincerely and faithfully." Yet, when we have all these, we are quick to forget our promise of love and service, with the result that these very blessings do us harm. That misfortunes are sent to us may then be put "shades of His Hand outstretched caressingly" to awaken us from our complacent torpor; the lash of stern compassion mercifully given. Our prayer was not a genuine lifting up of our real or imagined sorrows to God, but just a selfish whine to have things adjusted our way. We did not leave it to the inscrutable wisdom and infinite goodness of God to decide whether distress or prosperity, success or failure, life or death, was best in the interests of our eternal salvation. If, when we make our request, our intention is rather to force our own wishes on God than to abandon ourselves to His omniscient and merciful wisdom, then our petition is not a prayer but an act of arrogance and rebellion. We owe submission and adoration to God at all times; and most of all when we kneel to Him in our distress.

When we listen to the voice of conscience, we hear all these answers to our complaints about the inefficacy of the prayer of petition. But the essential reply to such complaints has been given us by God Himself, when He "emptied Himself, taking the form of a servant." Hanging on the cross, He too knew that moment of desolation when the Eternal Father seems to have left His human soul in desolation: "My God, my God, why hast thou forsaken me?" His coming among men "like unto them in all things, but without sin," was the answer to those ages of expectation wherein mankind had longed for Emmanuel, for God walking our ways. We have not, therefore, been harshly commanded to continue our prayer, with only the assurance that all will be righted on the Day of Judgment. Christ has come among us, to teach us how to pray, and to teach us the meaning of suffering. Through the Incarnation, the ecstatic prayer of the Son of God in the Bosom of His Father has become a human prayer on the lips of Christ, a prayer from the depths of the human misery and suffering of God made Man. In Christ, we find the true answer to the alleged inefficacy of prayer. He does not teach us the philosophy of prayer, nor does He discuss the conditions for prayer. We do not look to Him for the solution of those problems inherent in prayer: the readiness, for instance, we must show to accept God's answer to our petition, despite our longing that this answer should be the one we ourselves desire; the seeming paradox that, while prayer is efficacious, we cannot control the free decision of God in our regard; or, finally, the fact that, although we have been promised that prayers offered in the Name of Jesus will be heard, we find that so many of our prayers so offered go apparently unanswered. The great significant fact for us is that Christ taught us *how to ask* in prayer. Therefore, while we await in faith that Day of Judgment which will reveal all, we have Christ as our answer to all accusations against prayer. Our answer is that Christ of Whom the Scripture says: " In the day of his flesh, offering up prayers and supplications with a strong cry and tears to him that was able to save him from death, was heard for his reverence." (Heb. 5:7).

Christ has answered our questions by teaching us how to pray. He has taught us to pray in words of direct supplication, of holy confidence, of complete submission. His supplication was direct: " Remove this chalice from me." During His Agony in the Garden, He prayed with all the fervour of a man encompassed by terror and anguish. So earnest was His appeal that His sweat became as drops of blood. It pleased His infinite goodness to let us hear in His words the anguished cry of a *man*; for He did not ask for something sublime or heavenly, but for that mortal life to which we all cling so tenaciously. He shrank from the torture and disgrace He saw before Him, and asked His Heavenly Father to deliver Him from it. However, we know that He also spoke words which manifested complete confidence in His Father: "I know that thou hearest me always" (John, 11:42); and in the prayer of His agony, we are shown that complete submission which must animate all prayer: "Not my will but thine be done" (Luke 22:42). Apparently forsaken by His Father, tortured and crucified, He commended His soul into the Hands of His Father.

Let us consider how all this points to the great inner harmony in the Heart of Jesus. He wrestles with the Will of His Heavenly Father, and yet has entirely submitted to that Divine Will; He cries out in anguish, and yet is certain that He will be heard; He knows that He is heard always and in everything, and yet wishes to do nothing but the inscrutable Will of His Father; He begs for His life with the utmost urgency, and yet this prayer is an offering of His life to the Father. All these contrasts are harmonised in the prayer of Jesus, in a mysterious harmony wherein lies the secret of truly Christian prayer, because the prayer of God made Man is the model of Christian prayer. For as in Christ the Divinity and Humanity of Christ were united in one person, so human prayer and Divine prayer were united in the prayer of Christ.

A truly Christian prayer of petition is a prayer which is essentially human. We turn to God for His assistance in our fear of earthly distress, in our desire for protection, in our sorrows and sufferings. Such prayer is the cry of elementary self-preservation, a naked expression of our instinctive clinging to life, arising from the very depths of human life and human anguish. Yet, such prayer is also essentially divine. In the very act of, as it were, defending our earthly life against God, we adopt an attitude of complete submission to Him and to His inscrutable designs for us. We subordinate our instinctive self-preservation, wholly and unconditionally, to the Will of God, and we regard this Divine Will as the Source from which the final decision is to come. Thus, our prayer of petition is, in the ultimate analysis, not a plea for life and the things of this life, but a submission to the Will of God even when that Will points to deprivation and perhaps to death.

Such prayer is both human and divine. It is human,

in as much as it is a cry from the human heart in its misery and pain: it is divine in so far as it is an act of submission to the Divine Will. The more like our prayer is to that of Christ, the more vigorous, vital, and truly human it becomes. Thus transfused with the light and love of God, the earthly tribulations and desires which are the matter of our prayer are lifted to a higher plane, wherein they take on a higher significance as offerings of our submission to the Will of God. Such submission is a kind of divine alchemy by which both our failures and successes are transmuted to the pure currency that wins an eternal reward. By means of it, there is a mysterious fusion between the will of man and the Will of God—a fusion through which man is lifted to the heights of his true greatness. Christ has promised that all true prayer will be heard. He implements that promise always in the most exalted manner possible, by answering every prayer in accordance with the Will of God. The Divine Will of Christ is always at one with the Will of His Heavenly Father, and therefore the Father always hears Him. As children of the Father and brethren of Christ, we have been promised that our prayers too will be heard to the extent to which we identify our will with that of the Father. In other words, whatever our request, our ultimate wish must be that God may answer in such a way as to promote His own glory and increase His life in our souls. Such singlemindedness—" if thy eye be single," said Christ, " thy whole body will be lightsome "—casts out from our prayer of petition any shadow of selfish desire to make God's Will conform to ours, rather than ours to His; and thereby we become perfect children of God. While maintaining that freedom and autonomy of will which is our human prerogative, we yet establish with God a pure relationship of sympathy, a perfect harmony wherein we freely choose to submit our will to that of God. Thus, true to our nature, we may desire and pray for what we regard as conducive to our happiness; and yet know that we shall certainly receive the answer we desire, even in an apparent refusal of our request, because we desire only that the Will of God may be done.

We do not put all this forward as an explanation of the mystery of prayer, since it is simply a re-statement of the mystery of the Christian life in general. We explain the mystery of prayer by referring to the mystery of the whole Christian life; and though this may be to explain one mystery by another, nevertheless it is sufficient for one who has faith. Heaven and earth are realities. On the one hand, there is the Living, Free and Almighty God; on the other, there is the truly free nature of man, His creature. These two freedoms meet in prayer, wherein we find a cry of distress, a pleading for some good, coexisting with an attitude of complete submission to the inscrutable judgments of God. These two aspects—man's freedom to plead: man's submission to the free decision of God—are always found together in true prayer. "Unless you become as little children," said Christ—thereby pointing to the sublime virtue of Simplicity which is the essence of Christian perfection. To lead a truly Christian life is to place one's whole being into the Hands of God as confidently as a child takes the guiding hand of its father. The child's confidence is complete and without the slightest trace of reservation: the hand it grasps is of one who knows best, who loves, who will not lead it into any danger, who will shelter it from evil—but who certainly will not reach down that sharp knife or that poisonous liquid, however much the child, fascinated by the glitter or the colour, may clamour to have it. The profoundest secret of the Christian life and of Christian prayer is to become a child in our relations with God—a child whose quiet confidence and silent submission do not fail in moments of trial when God appears to have turned from us. Christ has given us the perfect example of this: "He went down to Nazareth and was subject" to Mary and Joseph, because it was the Will of His Father; He summed up His Public Life with the words —"I do not my own will, but the will of Him that has sent me"; and He ended His earthly life as One "obedient unto death, even unto the death of the cross." We have learnt from Him to plead with the the Father, but to find our peace of soul in the answer the Father mercifully gives.

This apology for prayer will be understood only by one who prays, for it is an understanding that can be reached only in the act itself of praying. We may indeed pray for material good—for necessities, for health; but always in such a way that our manner of asking redounds to our eternal glory, whatever the answer we receive. In asking, we must make an oblation of our will to that of God. We must pray with a constancy and perseverance which is a living proof of our trust in God's guidance of human affairs; of our hope in a world full of the shadows of death; of a true love for God which is not simply pious self-seeking and does not depend on incessant rewards. Since we are on this earth as "strangers and pilgrims" on a journey to eternity, we must not pray as though we had here "a lasting city." We know that it is through sickness and death that we shall enter into that life which is the final object of all our prayer. As long as we keep our minds raised to God in prayer, even when disappointments and misery crowd about us, we are sustained by the invisible and mysterious, yet true and real, power of God's grace and of participation in the life of God; and, when "this mind is in us," death loses its terrors and become a swallowing up in the abyss of God's everlasting love.

VI.

PRAYER OF DEDICATION.

PRAYERS of dedication play a great part in the private and public devotion of Catholics. Although this is not one of the oldest forms of prayer, it has now become so prevalent that it deserves some special consideration. We are familiar with the dedication of the world to the Sacred Heart pronounced in our churches e.g. on the Feasts of the Sacred Heart and of Christ the King. There is a similar dedication to the Immaculate Heart of Mary. We have the dedication of families to the Sacred Heart. Dioceses are dedicated by the bishops to a patron, or members of sodalities may dedicate themselves to their heavenly Patroness. The meaning and profundity of such dedications are subject to considerable variations according to the circumstances, the person to whom they are directed, the persons or communities who perform them, etc. However, we shall leave aside for the moment these differences; neither will we consider the official or liturgical aspects of some of these dedications. We shall confine ourselves to a consideration of the idea of dedication underlying such prayers, as found in the dedication of himself made by a person sincerely and on his own initiative.

Let us consider what exactly takes place in such a dedication. We know it is neither resolution nor vow. In the case of a resolution we resolve to do, or refrain from doing, something, in obedience to the commands or counsels given us by God. We put our own house in order; we are concerned with ourselves. In dedication, on the other hand, we do not primarily consider ourselves but the person to whom we dedicate ourselves. There is a transition from our heart to the heart of him to whom we dedicate ourselves.

In a vow we promise something specific to God, by imposing upon ourselves a new and strict obligation. This promise is certainly great and significant, since it is to result in a man's handing over of himself to the holy love of God. Thus, dedication to God is the ultimate aim of all vows. Yet, the immediate content of vows is certain clearly defined aims and efforts, while dedication goes straight from heart to heart. Dedication is not the choosing of a means of showing our love, a work in which love is to grow and to be tried, as in a resolution or a vow. Dedication is the free flow of love from person to person and heart to heart.

Is this something new? The Christian life should be always characterised by this flow of love, which extends not only to each single effort and good work, but to the whole of our existence. For this love is God's claim to our unconditional allegiance. Quite apart from the fact that many dedications are not directly addressed to God and Our Lord, do these dedications extend beyond a reiteration of what we already do, indeed what we are obliged to do, even without dedication? Dedication does not appear to be more than an echo of those quiet movements of the Holy Ghost which carry us gently and irresistibly unto God. Dedication cannot be a new obligation, because all old and all possible new obligations are always included in and anticipated by that love which, being higher than all duty, demands all from us. This love is fulfilled only when no boundaries are set to it: when, with our whole heart, we give our whole heart, a heart filled with love rather than with the idea of fulfilling a duty.

Yet, let us sound a warning at this point. Dedication concerns only what is always and everywhere our duty: I love Thee, my God. Does dedication add nothing to this? Is it of no added significance that these same words are now spoken earnestly from the heart, and with deliberation, where before they were perhaps lightly spoken without a deliberate conscious intention? In our spiritual life, there are surely prayers which are, as it were, its small talk. But dedication is seriously spoken: we put all that we are into our words, and see our future as bound by the dedication we are making. The current of our life goes on, apparently unchanged; but with a new, hidden, deeper significance.

It is through his spiritual life that a man strives for his ultimate goal, the perfection of his personality through the possession of God. This spiritual life is not a mere series of actions endlessly succeeding each other towards the attainment of a spiritual goal: the past exists mysteriously in every moment. Thus, as a spiritual being, man acts, or at least, can act, in every moment with the resoures of his entire past. His past is preserved in a concentrated form as the gathered experience of his life. The place from which a bullet was fired can be determined only by considering its whole path. Similarly a note sounded by a master violinist can be said to contain in essence that note as played by him up to the moment of its present perfection. In a far greater measure, the present action of a man embodies his whole past, his knowledge obtained through effort or through suffering, the depth of his experience, the revolutions of his life, his joys and his sorrows. Memory may modify these to some extent, but they are none the less present. By all these influences, the present action is given its direction, its depth and resonance. The past is preserved and carried forward in the present action. At least, that is how it ought to be. Into the present free decision, a person is called upon to gather up all the past, thus bringing to it all that he is and was—in other words the whole sum of his existence. Man must seize the successive possibilities offered to him, and in doing so, he realises what is eternal in him. Every moment is to be filled with his whole spiritual history, which to him is the ever more enriched possibility of present freedom.

It is still more mysterious, yet true, that in the grace of a present decision man can anticipate his future. This is not exclusive to such matters as resolution, planning, decision, premeditation, promise and vow, when man looks to the pattern of his future life. Besides, resolutions and similar spiritual and intellectual acts, remain in the present tense, however important they may be for the future of man: they become significant for the future only when actually carried

71

out, and this carrying out is subject to a subsequent rather than to a present decision. However, by saying that in a present action we can mysteriously anticipate the future, we mean something more than decisions which once taken cannot be altered, and therefore exercise an ineluctable influence on later conduct. There are such facts, and they vary in significance. Marriage and Holy Orders—indeed, even living through a certain unrepeatable period of our lives—create facts which exercise an influence on future actions and decisions. Any future action must take these facts into consideration, and a man can no longer act as if they did not exist. However, it is an equally important truth that a man can take these facts into consideration in very different ways. He can change the face of his decisions, e.g. he can either stand by his earlier decision to love a person, or he can betray this decision. His ordination to the priesthood can become more and more integrated into his life, or his life can be lived more and more outside his vocation, indeed he can become unfaithful to it. Thus the fact created in the past is not actually evaded, two opposite possibilities remaining after such facts have been created. For the future continues fundamentally undecided and undetermined. It is not this phenomenon to which we were referring when we said that the present moment can anticipate the future.

To explain what we mean, let us discuss an objection which might be put forward to disprove from the outset the possibility of such anticipation. Freedom seems to be incompatible with anticipation of the future. A man is always free. Therefore he is also free in the future moments of his life. Hence it is impossible that man should anticipate his future to such an extent that he decides it in the present moment, filling as it were the present moment with the import of the future and anticipating what is still in the future. The future cannot be realised in the present moment. It seems that at this point the words of Holy Scripture (Mat. 6:34) apply: "Sufficient for the day is the evil thereof."

One aspect of this objection is certainly to be maintained in our further considerations. Apart from exceptional cases to which we shall return later, the fact that in principle the entire life of man is free, means that in no case can the free decision of the moment decide the future in such a way that a man knows for certain and in a palpable manner that this decision has already shaped his future, and that thus the future has been decided here and now. If this were not so, the future would be an almost mechanical unfolding of what has happened in such a moment. Life would no longer be shadowed by the incalculable future, and would be no longer subject to the law of responsible initiative. Theology teaches us, and the history of the Saints bears out the truth, that there are cases in which a man can know, through a free and complete conviction reached in the sight of God, that his life has reached a stage where his salvation is already assured. This is what theologians term "confirmation in grace.' However, this is an exceptional case, which can be left aside at this stage, because it occurs but rarely and need not be considered with reference to our own life. In such confirmation in grace, man knows that, in a certain measure, his spiritual personality is already beyond the practical reach of sin.

As a general principle, such knowledge is not reconcilable with the freedom and uncertainty of our life on earth, where decisions are made in ignorance and in blind trust, due to the uncertainty of our insecure position in the face of God. Our question, therefore, is still unanswered. Is it possible to try to anticipate the future, even though the results of this venture may be uncertain? One reason for answering this question in the affirmative is that freedom is not essentially—as a common misconception would have it—the capacity to accomplish, at least by desire, whatever we wish to do here and now. The correct definition of freedom is a man's capacity to express his free personality completely, through decisions legitimately, freely and finally made. Freedom therefore does not deny the possibility of creating internal (as distinct from merely external) facts, which are definite and final. On the contrary, freedom has its ultimate meaning in this very possibility.

It is the very opposite of freedom to create conditions which are subject to alteration, change, reversion or revision. Freedom achieves unique and permanent finality. The ultimate, eternal destiny of the soul is not an accidental condition imposed on mankind as something which thwarts human freedom, as a foreign element which negates the very idea of that freedom. On the contrary, this destiny is the mature result of freedom itself. Therefore, at any moment a free decision can anticipate a man's entire life, since it can be decisive of his lot in eternity. Every moment of free decision exerts a shaping influence on the entire growth of human personality, since it is the complete expression of what a man really is within the depths of his own heart. There are many, of course, who make narrow decisions dictated by the expediency of the moment, rather than far-reaching decisions affecting their whole future and shaping their eternal destiny. Again, success often depends on external conditions outside the control of free will. A person may fail a thousand times in his attempts so to gather up all the possibilities of his spiritual life into one moment of decision, that all his future actions may receive a unifying significance from that decision. Yet the tendency to such decision is in us all, because it is part of the very essence of our freedom.

A truly free decision always reaches forward to the whole of our life and is decisive of our eternal destiny. In most cases, it will ultimately fail to sustain its effect, either because this free decision was too weak and therefore incapable of reaching down into the very springs of our being, or because external circumstances beyond our control were too much for us. It is scarcely possible to know with any degree of certainty whether our act of decision has completely succeeded in sustaining its effect. Nevertheless, in the moment of making such a decision, human freedom really expresses itself as a desire to influence our whole future, to shape that future to the image of our decision, and thus to reach its effect even into Eternity itself.

One such moment is inevitable. In death the thread of life is cut off, however much we might have liked to continue spinning the garment of our years. Although we never know how this can be done, and indeed although the appearances are inevitably against it, in death man completes his own pattern by dying his own death. In the moment of death he is what he has made of himself, freely and finally. The actual result of his life and what he wanted to be freely and finally, become as one. When exactly does death in the sense of this action of freedom, occur; and when does a man thus complete himself? What has been said of death is true in as much as, according to our faith, physical death is the free completion of man. However, we do not know whether this completion actually coincides in time with physical dissolution. What we know is that, apart from the exceptional cases to which we have referred, we can have no certainty that this moment of decision has been reached by us. Thus the moment of total decision lies always ahead of us, and we can only assume that it does not always coincide, and perhaps indeed very rarely coincides, with death in the physical sense. The approach of physical death is generally accompanied by a reduction of consciousness, and it is unlikely that in this state the total decision can be taken. Since any free action can in itself become an act of total decision, it is at least probable that such a moment of total decision takes place at a time other than that of physical death. Since this total decision is the basic aim of freedom, we should indeed prepare for it at any moment.

What has so far been theoretically deduced from the nature of freedom is confirmed by experience. In the history of our own soul, we remember moments which seemed indeed unforgettable. The experience, disposition and intention felt by us at that moment seemed to be destined to remain deeply rooted within us. We realised that we could never go back on what we had freely chosen in that moment, for the very reason that the choice was free. Advancing in age, we are sometimes overcome, gently and softly but with unspeakable rapture, by some awareness of the grace of God taking possession of us. The Divine Huntsman will see to it that His game does not escape Him. Our soul merely waits for the moment when His love will seize upon us finally. Let us not forget that such awareness of grace is an action involving our freedom, because it evokes a consent from the very depths of our being.

Even when such awareness proves to be an illusion, the very fact of this illusion seems to indicate our belief that there exists in reality what then appeared to us. When the mountaineer thinks he has reached the summit, a new stretch of the path opens up before his eyes, a stretch which was not yet visible when he estimated the distance he still had to cover. The illusion, in an individual case, merely proves that our soul has been created for such moments when everything is finally completed. Suddenly, unexpectedly and without any warning, there will come upon us what we had always hoped for, the fullness of life caught up in one moment of decision, the expression of freedom in its final perfection.

In freedom, we anticipate the whole unity of our life. Again and again, our anticipation will seize upon only a fraction of the whole, but we will not cease in our efforts to gather up past and future into that one decision of freedom from which our life will receive its final and definite truth and reality. Only God will hear when the hour of our glory strikes: unexpectedly and without knowing it ourselves, the fruits of our whole life will be in our hands. Whatever happens afterwards in our life is but an exultant Finale of a symphony, the final count in an election whose result is beyond doubt, the ripening of a fruit after it has been gathered.

Let us call this great hour of our freedom, the unique and undisguised presence of the moment of eternity in time, the moment of "temporal eternity". The nature of this moment appears to us in a dark manner: indeed, being the fruit of freedom, the moment itself remains hidden. We know that it is of the nature of freedom to strive for this moment which is its fulfilment. Whether we are aware of it or not, we are always living in the attempt to reach this moment of fulfilment.

So far, we have endeavoured to determine the moment of "temporal eternity" in its abstract form as the act by which a man disposes of himself and of all the possibilities of his life. The content of this act, however, is still undetermined. This act of freedom can be one thing or another, Yes or No, ascent or descent, salvation or damnation, everlasting gain or eternal lose. Let us therefore try to determine the full content of this moment, if it is indeed to be everlasting salvation, pure and final affirmation. It is through the love of God that man succeeds in his attempt to secure his happiness in eternity. This definition is far from being self-evident. It is clear that not every act of the love of God is a moment of what we have called "temporal eternity". Every act of the love of God may be an attempt to achieve our unique moment of eternity in time; but only in very rare cases will we know with certainty whether we have succeeded in this attempt. In fact, except for one attempt, all these attempts are bound to fail. Needless to say, these failures are by no means insignificant in the eyes of God or for ourselves; they are important and indeed indispensible exercises leading up to the supreme effort.

The identification of the act of love and the moment of eternity in time cannot take place unless we enter into it with our whole heart, our whole soul, our whole mind and strength, that is to say, unless we entirely spend ourselves in this act of loving freedom, making it final and irrevocable. Such an act of love can be attained but rarely, indeed only once, and this for ever. When did we ever love God with our whole heart, our whole soul, our whole mind and all our strength (Mark 12:30)? If we could fully understand the terrifying meaning of the words "whole" and "all", we would see that the commandment to love God with our entire being amounts to a commandment to direct our entire life towards the achievement of that moment of eternity in time. Our life would then be a continuous effort, until this grace is given to us. To strive for this success, in the moment of eternity in time, is the commandment of love. Every act of love tends towards that moment, in which it finds its fulfilment; but not every act of love is yet that unique moment.

In still another respect, it is not immediately evident that an act of love or indeed any human act can indeed be the true moment of eternity in time. We have said that in this moment an integration of our whole life takes place. It is by no means self-evident how love, and love only, is able to bring about this integration. Indeed at this point we realise how little we really know about what we call Love. Which is the fundamental act into which a man can gather up his whole essence and his whole life? Which is the act that embraces everything, that comprehends everything and contains everything human, our laughter and tears, bliss and despair, mind and heart, everyday life and our moments of supreme happiness, compulsion and freedom, sin and redemption, past and future? We hesitate to answer this question: and yet, the answer is clear. The love of God, and only the love of God, embraces everything. It brings a man face to face with Him without Whom he could experience nothing but a terrifying consciousness of emptiness and negation. The love of God alone unites all powers in man—manifold, chaotic and contradictory as they are—and directs them to God. The One and Infinite God alone can create in man that unity which binds together what is manifold and contradictory without destroying it. Love alone makes man forget himself, and it would indeed be hell if such self-oblivion could never be achieved. Love alone can redeem even the darkest hours of the past, since love alone is brave enough to believe in the mercy of God. Love alone does not selfishly hold back: it is therefore able to dispose even of the future. Without love, man, anxiously guarding his finite Ego, would husband his future and yield it but grudgingly. Love alone can, as it were, draw God on to this earth, thus integrating all earthly love in the moment of eternity. To love alone, therefore, is given that persistency of courage which loves Him Who sees, through guilt, failure and death, the bravery of His creature. The love of God is really the only total integration of human existence. Its sublime dignity and all-embracing greatness become clear to us when we understand this point. The full content of the moment of "temporal eternity" cannot be anything else, because without the love of God that moment would be nothing more than the secret judgment (John 3:18) and because conversely, only in that moment can the love of God be what it desires to be and what it must be.

Much more could be said of this act of love in the moment of eternity in time. Above all, we must bear in mind that this act is grace, although it is the most sublime act of freedom. This moment is grace, because we can love God only in His strength and power, because our love is only the response to His love, and because there is no love in us other than that which His Holy Spirit has poured out into our hearts. This moment is pure grace as such, because it transcends all the general grace of the love of God. It is given only to the Angels to be free at any moment to surrender entirely, to seize the very depth of all possibilities, and to smelt the core of life that it may be used without dross for the casting of a true image of God. Men are given this possibility only in those supreme moments of their lives granted to them by grace, when this possibility is given to them in such a way that they can really fulfil it. It is by grace that this moment is given to them, and it is by the super-abundance of grace that this moment is given to them in such a way that they can fill it with the love of God. Thus the highest moment of freedom is essentially both grace and freedom; in that moment, freedom determines itself in the everlasting integration of an entire life.

We seem to have strayed far away from our initial question concerning the nature of dedication. Yet, our goal is at hand. We can now define dedication as the earnest attempt to reach the moment of eternity in time through an act of love. We will readily see that this definition is true when we consider our definition of the moment of eternity in time as the act of total and final integration of our whole life, and when we compare this definition with our experience of what is done in dedication. It requires no further proof that dedication is fundamentally an act of love. The very externals of dedication reveal its nature as a pure and recollected act involving the whole strength of our being, uniting all the powers of the mind and the heart, deliberately and earnestly. What else is the preparation, the solemnity, and the explicit and deliberate form of dedication?

It will have now become clear that such an act of love strives by its very nature to bring about the moment of eternity in time, because only in that moment does love well up from the very depths of the heart. Dedication as such implies that there is the possibility of success in this effort. Such success means that the moment of eternity in time occurs, as, in the eyes of God, the decisive event in our life, the act to which our previous life was the mysterious prelude. That moment is the object, goal and end; what follows is but the working out of the theme irrevocably adopted. This attempt will frequently end in failure or at least only in partial success, and we will never know whether and how far it has been successful. After our dedication, therefore, we will have to continue to strive earnestly for our salvation, conscious of the fact that we are not yet what we are to be and what we are called to be. The pilgrimage will continue, perhaps for a long time, and it will hold many surprises. Yet, even as an attempt, dedication is holy and great. No one knows but the attempt may have been successful. Perhaps the decisive word has been spoken—the word in which we have borne witness to what we are. *We* do not know, but *He* knows. Let it suffice. It is in the nature of love to seek ever for new words, more intimate, more sincere and more earnest still, until the word is found that really expresses everything and for ever.

We may wish to consider the manner in which dedications should be performed. It cannot be an everyday event in our spiritual life. It requires preparation. It needs some consideration of the intellectual, mental and spiritual properties of him who dedicates himself, so that his heart is really in the words of dedication. It would be wrong to multiply dedications, since dedication must be the result of an earnest and realistic representaion of our whole life. We must pray for true dedication as a gift of grace. However, we cannot consider these aspects more fully here.

This chapter started with the question of what takes place in dedication, and we can now attempt to answer this question. Dedication is the attempt to consecrate in some way the whole of life. If this attempt is successful, it is not just an achievement, but the totality of all achievement. If this attempt is not completely succcessful, something of supreme importance has nevertheless been achieved: a part of that love has been realised which in any case is the task of this life and the meaning of eternity. Someone may say that this is done every day of the Christian life, because the monotony and bitterness of everyday life is the true theatre of love. Quite true, if everyday life is really love. As everyday life is not, by nature, love, it is wholesome and good that what *should* be done always, *is* actually, expressed and deliberately done on certain occasions. Such occasions are dedication, even where we do not succeed in bringing the fullness of love into the moment of eternity in time. In dedication, therefore, everything, or at least something very important, is achieved.

So far we have looked upon dedication from the point of view of man. Let us now ask whether in dedication something is done by God. Let us consider His answer to the word of love spoken in dedication. This answer given by God is indeed the very essence of what is done in dedication. The Scripture says: " Draw nigh to God and He will draw nigh to you " (James 4:8). We should say more of the nearness of God and His splendour as experienced in dedication. Yet, the decisive point has already been made: He approaches to us by giving us the grace to approach to Him. The meaning of this approach to and by God has been discussed throughout this chapter.

So far, our considerations have been based on the assumption that we treat of dedications to God the Father, the Holy Trinity, to the Love of God made-Man and to His Sacred Heart. We have spoken of the highest moments of the love of God when it is directed to God Himself. Let us briefly consider dedications to the saints, especially to the Blessed Virgin, rather than to God directly. If we have rightly understood the meaning of dedication, it will be obvious to us that such indirect dedications to God are covered by our definition. Such dedications, as acts of love to a human being now assumed into the community of God in heaven, are essentially acts of the love of God. Love of our neighbour—and one eternally united to God is in a special way our neighbour —is directed towards God, since it is an expression of the theological virtue of Charity. Why this is so and how this can be so, requires no explanation, but has been extensively discussed by theologians. In dedication to a human being in heaven, our heart does not centre on him, but we unite ourselves with that purity of soul through which he has won eternal bliss. By this means, we sanctify our prayers and our actions, giving them a power more than their own. This concerns in particular dedications to the Blessed Mother of God and to her Immaculate Heart, the living symbol of her love of God, the symbol of the totality of her purity and her complete surrender to the Will of God in eternal love. He who dedicates himself to this love and really understands what he is doing, will be irresistibly drawn into the eternal movement of love in the Immaculate Heart of Mary. In this act of love, he loves God; and his dedication is to God through Mary.

Many different prayers of dedication have been said on our behalf and by us. Sometimes they may have appeared to us all too frequent. We may feel uncomfortable at the way in which they use the loftiest words, since such words seem so far in excess of our real feelings. There may be cases in which he who truly loves God prefers to remain silent, content with offering to God his sincere desire of that love of which his cold heart comes short. We may feel that there is no need to declare our love to Him who reads our hearts. Still, we must reassure ourselves of this love, and God in His love knows the weakness of our heart. His Divine Love accepts from us even that love which is not worthy of Him. He loves in us that diffidence which makes us distrust our love and our ability to love. It is perhaps part of our unredeemed pride that, although we know how God loves us, we remain silent in modesty and fear rather than speak like children. This pride implies fundamentally that our love could be worthy of Him, and that He loves us truly only when our love is as it should be. Let us abandon this pride. Let us speak to Him as children, confidently and earnestly: " My Father, I dare to tell Thee that I love Thee." All prayers of dedication are but expositions and variations of this one inexhaustible theme.

VII.

PRAYER FOR FORGIVENESS.

"WHEN thou shalt pray, pray in this manner: Our Father, . . . forgive us our trespasses." (Matth. 6:6 and 9). Having thus learned how to pray, a Christian prays every day for the forgiveness of his sins. Let us pray for this intention every day and with renewed fervour. Let us not pray merely for the forgiveness of former sins, of sins committed at the time prior to our conversion, when we had not yet repented and when perhaps we were not yet sanctified by the forgiveness of sins through our re-birth by water and the Holy Ghost. Let us pray ceaselessly for the forgiveness of that guilt of sin which is ours here and now.

However, we do not really feel our guilt to such an extent that every day we could strike our breast in the spirit of true repentance, saying with a contrite heart: "Lord, have mercy upon me, a poor sinner." Moreover, we are redeemed children of God, whose very countenance should be suffused with the glory of redemption. We are the joyful heirs of the saints in light, the re-born children of the Father, shining like stars in a world of darkness. We are the children of mercy, the new people, the heirs of His promise.

In general, Christians nowadays become conscious of their faith only many years after their Baptism. Baptism marks the beginning of a man's spiritual life. In Baptism the mercy of God appears at the beginning of his pilgrimage, before that pilgrimage has properly started. This position of Baptism is justified when we consider what is the part played by God in our life, and what the part left to ourselves. Still, Baptism does not exempt us from running our course, from fighting against the powers of darkness and the onslaughts of temptation. We cannot evade the great and decisive task laid on us by our Baptism: to become Christians, that is, to accept God by a free decision of our innermost being, with our whole heart and mind.

We must go forward to meet the majesty and the incomprehensible mercy and grace of God, Who appeared to us in Christ, was revealed on the Cross, and shone forth in the Ascension and in the Descent of the Holy Ghost. In this encounter between God and man, which, beginning with our Baptism, will decide our fate in life everlasting, there is a phase in which man strays away from God in the vanity of his heart as if the flesh and the earth were his ultimates. In this situation, a man may appear to be a perfectly normal and decent individual, who never gets into trouble with the police or transgresses the easy code of accepted day-to-day social conduct. However, in this situation, he remains unaware of the consuming holiness of God. Partly guilty, partly innocent, he trespasses against the commandments of the Lord which decide life and death. He does not realise how seriously he should regard the life of man, the waywardness of youth, and the concessions which advanced age makes to the demands of life, concessions between what ought to be and what is considered as unfortunately inevitable. There are the years in which he turns away from his Church, saying that he does not know how he slipped into this retrogression. Shrugging his shoulders, he contents himself with a bare statement of the fact that faith no longer exists for him.

In this situation he may be overtaken, as in olden times some men were overtaken before their Baptism, by the grace of God. The judgment of God may come upon him, tearing down the mask he has assumed, showing him what he is. Despite his denial, he has always known in the depths of his heart what he really is: a sinner loving darkness more than light, and easily accommodating his standards of conduct to the demands of his own wishes. He admits that he consented to his retrogression, even if he did not actually bring it about. It was not his fault if he unwittingly turned off the alarm clock of conscience that he might sleep out his life without a feeling of guilt. Imperceptibly, he had moved away from God. He could not stand the presence of God, a fact which seemed to prove to him that God does not exist, or at least no longer exists in the way he first envisaged Him. His complacency had appeared to him as a sign of a good conscience, though he admitted the theoretical possibility that his conscience might be wrong. Overtaken by the judgment of God, this idea collapses. He realises that his so-called good conscience proves the depth to which free and therefore truly guilty sin has affected him to the very core. Sin had so taken possession of him that in his heart there was no longer any voice warning him.

That this internal light of true conscience was extinguished is then no longer an excuse, but on the contrary is the clearest proof of his love of darkness. He no longer sees the light that enlightens every man, and is the result of the incomprehensible grace of God. Perhaps, for some time, he will fight the new light, defending his former " good conscience " or even turning the new light into a reproach against God. He will say that God should have shown him the light earlier, and he will not admit that it was he himself that refused to see, perhaps in order to avoid a real break with and full condemnation of his former life. Though he has now received a new and better understanding, he still wishes to maintain an unbroken continuity in his life. He will try to shelter in excuses by saying that he always meant well, though he did not always succeed too well. He will claim that his road followed a straight line as laid out for him from the beginning, and that he really remained true to this line.

However, when the sweet and burning light of God, the truth of God rather than of man, and the love of God, continue their inexorable and divinely inscrutable persistence, he will yield. In thus yielding, he finds his strength. He is given courage to relinquish his false freedom, and accept the dictates of a true conscience. In these dictates, he recognises the judgment of a merciful God. He admits that he is a sinner. He admits his guilt, and no longer excuses himself by saying that he did not know. He no longer claims that it was by a natural development that he found his way back to God, and that fundamentally he had never lost his innocence. No, he sincerely admits his guilt. He realises that in the depths of his heart there had been evil, and that he had deliberately evaded the whole issue by cultivating a false conscience which he knew would give him the answers he wished to hear. He had forgotten God, and he no longer claims that he had forgotten "accidentally". His corrupted heart had suggested "good" reasons to his mind, misnaming them "intellectual difficulties". He had been overcome by his inclination to evil because fundamentally he had sided with it long before it had made any specific demands on him. He was a sinner, fighting a continuous rear guard moral action, to prevent the cowardice of the final capitulation from becoming all too apparent. He had only too readily permitted the birds of passage of this age to steal the seed of God from the soil of his heart, because he wanted to escape the effort of bringing forth good fruit. He had been very clever in inventing ingenious moral principles of his own, dictated by the need of the moment or coming to him as veritable "inspirations", and enabling him to do with an easy conscience whatever he wished. He had been a man who said to God: "Give me good advice, as long as this advice falls in with my wishes. Let me have a good conscience such as will enable me to yield peacefully to temptation."

Now, a splendid transformation has taken place. Enlightened by God, he admits that he had nourished in his heart wickedness masked as light. He no longer asks how this could have come about in his heart, but confesses that he is himself its author. Speaking to God, he no longer tries to cloak his guilt like the Samaritan woman at Jacob's well. He does not shelter any longer behind a delusion of impersonal guilt. By the grace of God, he renounces himself. Nothing remains in him, when once he has renounced his former way of thinking, that would deserve the punishment of hell. God has saved him for the sake of that last spark of goodness that remained alive. In this transformation, man flees from himself rather than from God. He witnesses against himself where before he put up a defence; and thus he promotes the glory of God. Carried over the abyss by Divine grace, he is at one with God. The judgment of God is His mercy. He begins to love God, and because of this love he need not hate himself any longer. The miracle of grace has occurred: he is enamoured of the love of God, because he now recognizes that his very denial of that love was the dark prison of self to which he had been condemned by his own insincerity. Thus, he really comes to pray:

" Father, I have sinned against Thee. Forgive my sins."

This transformation, however, does not yet answer our initial question whether he who is honest and is redeemed can recite every day a prayer for the forgiveness of his sins. We still want an answer which applies to all of us and to every day. It will be said that one redeemed from the darkness of his own guilt into the Light of God will again and again confess his guilt, this confession being the profession of love by a sinner redeemed, liberated and restored to happiness. Though given to us by God, grace remains His property. He who has truly received grace, who is pure in himself, and who has been restored to the liberty of love, never claims the Divine glory of his new life as his own achievement. He never claims it as his well-deserved right. Grace remains grace, depending on the ever renewed miracle of the love God bears to us. It can never be regarded as something that has an existence independent of the generosity of God. Only as so dependent, is it man's new life. It is grace only as long as it is received as the ever renewed embrace by which the prodigal is forgiven. Is it in fact renewed or is it continuous and permanent? The sequence of time disappears in this act that covers a man's whole life. By grace, man is lifted from the most profound depths of his guilt to an equally profound union with God. Man must always say: " I am a sinner," because God always says: " Thou art the child of my love." But, through the creative love of God, the human truth that a man is a sinner, is reversed by God's truth that he is a child of God, and therefore cannot be fundamentally a sinner. This transformation can take place, however, only through God and through mans' prayer for His mercy.

Those who have but a superficial knowledge of general practice might be inclined to say that a good Christian indeed prays every day for the forgiveness of his daily faults and weaknesses. These venial sins do not separate him from God, and in spite of them he remains a child of God. Still, they are sins. Despite the miracle of grace, he will fall seven times daily, as the Scripture warns us; and therefore it is not as supererogation, but as a necessity, that even the saints ask for the forgiveness of their sins. All this is true, but it is not the whole truth.

Venial sins must, of course, be taken seriously, and must not be considered too trivial to require forgiveness. We must understand the meaning of the word " slight " applied by moral theologians to venial sin, and we shall have more to say later on the seriousness of these sins. Yet, the daily prayer of a good Christian, of a Christian in the state of grace, is not solely concerned with actual venial sin. It is not conducive to praying for forgiveness from the bottom of our heart, to consider only our venial sins. In fact, we have here one of the great sources of spiritual dishonesty, abhorrent to the Lord in our prayers. Confining ourselves to the consideration of actual venial sins and assuming, as taught by the Church, that they are but slight sins, we are not brought to that deep heart, that profundity of conviction, wherein a man really grapples with himself and wherein his eternal destiny is decided. The consideration of venial sins only touches the fringe, however revealing these sins may be as regards our true spiritual state and however voluntary they may have been in the strict sense of freedom. Accordingly, such sins cannot be the subject of a contrition deeper than their own nature. Contrition as the reaction of the heart to venial sin, cannot plumb the depths of a man, because it cannot be more serious than the venial sins themselves. An attempt to take them more seriously leads to dishonesty and is a dangerous strain on our spiritual potentialities. It may result in narrowing down the difference between venial and grievous sin, and, since venial sins cannot be avoided altogether but must be accepted to some extent as inevitable, we are in danger of losing the proper perspective also with regard to mortal sin. Experienced confessors know that the indiscriminate confession of mortal and venial sins shows this to be a very real danger. Venial sins can be the subject of regret. We can and should strive to avoid them. They show us how little we are fundamentally directed towards God and how little we have ' put on the new man '. We may be terrified at the possible developments of our character as adumbrated by our venial sins, which make us fear for our salvation. We may measure by them how far we are from that inner harmony of spirit effected in us by the love of God our Saviour. We must reject venial sins,

Thy will be done!
O my God, for the Church,
for your priests and for souls

SUFFERING
IN THE SERVICE
OF THE HOLY CHURCH

Merciful Jesus, Who, through love of us hast saved humanity, by suffering and dying upon the Cross, graciously accept through the Mother of Sorrows, my life of suffering for the salvation of the world.

Receive the offering of my cross, united with yours, in order to make fruitful the ministrations of your priests, and to hasten throughout the world the coming of your Reign of Light, of Love, and of Peace.

Thy will be done! O my God, for the Church for your priests and for souls.

Imprimatur : Frib. Helv. die 10 Maii 1966
R. Pittet, v.g.

because they cannot be positively reconciled with the perfect keeping of the commandments of God bidding us to strive for our only and eternal goal. They keep us in opposition to—or, as Aquinas said, at a distance from—the will of God. They reveal a deficiency in zealous love of God, and we must overcome this deficiency by a new effort of the heart. All this, however, does not stir hearts to their depths in realization of the words of God: "Thou art a sinner." We are not pierced by the sword separating body and soul, entering right into the centre of our heart. By confining ourselves to venial sins, we make these words apply where the real sin is not, and we thus escape the necessity of passing judgment upon our innermost intentions.

When said by those redeemed in the spirit, and by the saints, the words: "Forgive us our trespasses" have a totally different significance. Spoken in tears, in fear and terror, these words apply to something other than venial sins alone. Precise and correct though it is in moral theology, the term "venial sin" becomes fraught with danger when not considered in direct relationship to the sinner's entire personality.

What, then, is the meaning of the prayer for forgiveness as literally intended even by the saints, but not restricted merely to daily faults and negligence, nor to those venial sins due to our imperfect union with God?

Let us consider this point in the light of the teaching of Catholic theology. We have said that a man can be convicted by God of being a sinner. A man is made to realise that he personally, rather than men in general and everywhere, has sinned and has decided against God. Deceiving himself, he may not admit that it was he himself, unique, irreplaceable and fully responsible as he is, that trespassed. The realization of this fact is of overwhelming terror to the Ego. At last, a man can no longer claim to be other than a sinner. He cannot flee from himself, unless he tries to escape from God. He must condemn himself. He tries to save himself by sophistry: to minimise his sin, he magnifies the sin to a disease affecting all men, and of which he is the unfortunate victim. He does not say: "I have sinned against God," without hiding behind the thought that others have done likewise; but he says: "Truly, man everywhere and always is a sinner, always and in everything; he is fundamentally evil in Thy sight, O God. Man is a sinner by the very fact that, being man, he is different from Thee. Even before he begins to think, he finds he has decided against God. Man cannot escape from his guilt, and it remains his personal guilt; to try to escape is mere useless pride, attempting to justify itself in the eyes of God rather than confess its universal guilt." Thus, actual and concrete sin, committed in a definite set of circumstances, with full advertance and full consent, is impersonalised and made to appear as sin in its abstract essence. Actual sin seeks shelter behind original sin, by claiming to be an accidental and inevitable manifestation of original sin.

In this way, the nature of sin seems to be understood in a more radical sense. It is generalised. Its beginning is seen as prior to the actual trespass. Actual sin is dissolved into the past. It becomes quite natural to issue a decree to everyone: "Confess that you are a sinner." However, the individual tries to hide in the multitude, so that the confession of personal sin is swallowed up in the general intoning of the sombre *Miserere* of all men.

This condition is far from the truth. Catholic teaching is that my guilt is due to my individual action and is a new fall of Adam—however much, as a son of Adam, I may plead that I bear my father's burden; each time I must reckon with the possibility that others have had no part in my personal sin. Each one of us must confess that he was not compelled to commit this sin, that he could have avoided it and that, when he had committed it, it was his sole responsibility. There can be no deeper explanation than the personal admission that I have sinned, rather than the abstract admission that I am a sinner. This admission must not be the beginning of a flight from the sophistry of evil in my own heart. Our sin is scaled down to its real proportions by our admission that it was we who have committed it. Not even in the eyes of God, is everyone "fundamentally" like ourselves; others did not sin, where we have sinned; we alone have sinned and that sin is ours alone. Nothing else can be included by a man in such confession except sin, his own sin; and this he must radically reject. Only in this way will he attain to truth.

In this specific and personal confession, we understand anew what it means to be a creature. This confession, leading to the abandoning of ourselves, is indeed impregnated by the love of God. Where no personal and actual sin is committed and the white garment of baptismal grace has been kept unstained unto the judgment seat of Christ, there is still nothing but grace, pure grace, and indeed grace in more than usual abundance. The grace of Divine life is given to the creature as an unmerited gift. It is even more unmerited since we share in the sin of our first parents. It is solely due to our redemption through Christ. Moreover, any decision in which the grace of God might have been lost had it not been taken in such a way that we did not after all forfeit our inheritance, is in itself grace, as is every right and inspired action resulting from our free will. Those who have never sinned are nevertheless saved purely by grace. It was not they themselves that avoided falling into the abyss of guilt, but it was God who prevented them from falling. He holds us in our freedom. Our freedom is not such that the Almighty cannot act until it has vanished.

St. Irenaeus says that he who remains from the beginning in the love of God is a hymn of praise to the inscrutable grace of God. Like the worst sinner, he remains with God only by continual fleeing from himself and from his occasions of sin. There is nothing that we have not received. The more we have, the more we are indebted to God. The purest innocence leaves us the greatest debtors of God, and this debt is paid only in praising Him for His ineffable grace, and in confessing that everything is His work.

Thus there is the theoretical possibility of being free of sin, though we do not know, except in the case of the Handmaid and Mother of the Redeemer, whether any have been preserved from sin, and if so, how many. God alone knows what redemption is, and the redemption of each of us is His secret. How truly then can we say: "I am a sinner," since no one may say he is free from sin. St. John writes: " If we say that we have not sinned, we make him a liar and his word is not in us " (I. John 1 : 10). Whatever may be the meaning of these words, if no one may claim to be free of sin, must each one admit

91

that he has committed sin, even though he cannot remember having ever done so? Or if he does not admit to sin, is he necessarily a stubborn liar refusing to confess and to surrender to God? Is he always inspired by a cowardice and a pride which refuses to admit that God is in the right? Or is there something savouring of presumption in an excessive readiness to admit that I have sinned, and this merely to be at peace with Him Who is always right?

A point can be reached where the words: " I confess that I am a sinner " are equivalent to: " I do not say that I am not a sinner." In the latter case the judgment is left to God; in the former, it is assumed by man. The latter is possible, but the former is not always possible. A man may be genuinely unaware that he has committed any sin, and yet not be justified by this knowledge; and God can have mercy as He wills, keeping us from sin or snatching us from sin, preserving us or raising us. Of course, there are cases, indeed innumerable cases, in which a man, while leaving the final judgment to God Who alone knows our hearts, must say simply and honestly: " I have sinned." This confession, then, is something we can make both in the eyes of God and of the Church. It is made from the conviction of a conscience which honestly states the facts and admits the truth. This confession, made in strict sincerity before God and his Church, is a man's only honest expression of the glory of Divine grace. If, however, this confession is not possible owing to the fact that the person is genuinely unaware of any sin, the rejection of such a confession, out of respect for human sincerity and truth, does not amount to the claim that one is not a sinner. " For if I am not conscious to myself of anything: indeed in this I am not justified: but he that judgeth me is the Lord " (I. Cor. 4 : 4). If in thanksgiving for the grace of God, I dare to say, in fear and awe, that I am not conscious to myself of anything, I do not necessarily presume to be justified in the eyes of God. Regarding himself, a man can say, soberly and realistically, that he has fought a good fight and that he has kept faith and charity. Lifting up his eyes to God and kneeling down before Him, he will add: " If thou wilt mark iniquities, Lord, who shall stand it." (Ps. 129 : 3).

God alone knows what is in man. No man knows, with a certainty that requires nothing but Divine confirmation, whether his unselfishness is merely a refined form of egotism, whether his meekness is merely weak cowardice, whether his purity is mere physical impotence, whether his faith is escape into facile security and cheap sentimentality, and whether his general conduct is merely "decorum". We have become aware of the dark powers hidden in the depths of our soul. Our daily sins assume a new complexion and a greater weight when they reveal to us that everything *is* in us and everything is *possible* in us and through us. Thus we cannot assert that our Ego, acting, deciding and bearing the ultimate responsibility in the eyes of God, is to be located in that inextricable maze of contradictory forces, at the precise place where it can be identified with that force which testifies in us against darkness and for God. Standing before God rather than in the marketplace of life, we cannot say with ultimate certainty whether what is good in us is merely the mask concealing evil, and whether the evil in us has really been conquered. No one knows what really to make of himself in his poor distracted heart; whether his real self lives in his longing for a greater love of God, or in his unacknowledged and unrepentant grumbling at the immeasurable demands of this love. We long for simplicity: to see our twisted and tortuous selves with that clear directness with which God sees us. But this is impossible for us.

The most exalted goodness can pervert itself to the grimmest evil with the speed of lightning. Paradise was the scene of the most abominable fall. Even the elected messengers of God may be deluded by the belief that they can promote the glory of God by obeying the guidance of their own light rather than the testimony of the Son of God. "I saw Satan fall like lightning from heaven," was Christ's solemn warning to the Apostles when He heard them presuming on their own fitness for the Kingdom of Heaven. No man can claim that he is justified before God: his daily sins rise up to testify against him; and though these may be but venial, he must recognise them as pointers to the deep insubordination of his heart. Radical wickedness need not always reveal its presence conspicuously and outwardly. Should a man say, though he is not aware of having committed any sin: " I am a sinner "? How else can he express concisely and plainly the truth about himself and about what he is apart from the grace of God, which is always present as the active principle of goodness? It is by God that a man is upheld and saved; it is through himself that a man is lost; it is to himself that a man is a mystery. He can be judged only by God, and in this judgment there is but one confession, that contained in the word "sinner". O Lord, Thou knowest everything. Thou knowest me, a sinner, and Thou knowest the love that Thou workest in me.

What man really is, he is already in this life. In spite of his miserable inadequacies and in spite of all future possibilities from new decisions, he is what he really is in the eyes of God: for all things concerning him are " naked and open " to the eyes of God, even though they may be a tangled confusion to the man himself. How is it that we do not know ourselves, although we are clearly aware of the actions we freely do, and of how they must appear to God? In order to preserve the ambiguity of our present state, do we attempt to hide in a twilight which blurs the definite lines of free responsible action, although our salvation clearly depends on such action and indeed is decided by it?

To answer this question, we must know what " certain knowledge " about ourselves we have excluded, and what " lack of knowledge " we have cultivated, before we can decide whether we deserve love or wrath. We have ruled out reflection and introspection, because we have recognised once and for all that these do not give us certain knowledge of ourselves. In this field, we cannot allow simplification in accordance with theories that achieve clarity at the expense of completeness. In the spiritual, as in every other sphere, introspection is of little value to us in establishing the precise condition of our interior state. We cannot observe a thing or an action without immediately beginning to reflect upon it; and in so doing, we change the thing itself or the action itself, because such reflection is not a passive process of objective examination, but adds a foreign element of significant judgment. It is then no longer the thing or the action which is being considered, but the thing or the action as coloured by our own minds. This in turn demands further analysis, and so the process of endless reflection goes on. It has been suggested that this process is like that of a self-conscious golfer trying *not* to see himself posing to hit the ball; an attempt which immediately involves him in the problem of *not seeing* himself *not seeing* himself posing to hit the ball . . . and so on endlessly. However accessible, necessary and useful introspection may be, it cannot give us a complete prelogical, *objective* verdict on our actions. One process of introspection must necessarily lead to another, and we can have no guarantee that each process is not vitiated by a desire to hoodwink ourselves—by a manipulation of the figures, so to speak, that the answer may come out as we ourselves wish. The more elaborate the introspection, the less lucid is the result yielded likely to be; and there is no degree of reflection which can guarantee us certain knowledge of ourselves. A man realizes himself only through union with something outside himself, but he cannot *become* that " something." We can therefore have no clear and self-evident knowledge of ourselves. To some extent, the explanatory springs of our conduct remain hidden in the unconscious. Hence the Council of Trent specifically declared that no one can say with absolute certainty that he is in the state of grace.

Yet there is some sort of knowledge—or whatever name we give to the light that is compatible with action—by which we can distinguish what we are now doing from what we have done in the past, and by which we recognise our responsibility towards God. It may be expressed by a man's saying that he *knows* provided he is not asked how he knows. The judgment of God will uncover the hidden recesses of our heart and will confound mere introspection; while our heart will admit that at bottom it always knew what now comes to light. This knowledge was indeed knowledge of myself, and therefore could not be clarified by subjective reflection. It is only when a man has turned to God that this clear knowledge, which eludes all introspection, emerges clearly and compellingly. It cannot be translated in terms of what we usually call knowledge. Man can judge himself only in his actions.

Nevertheless, there is that peculiar knowledge which may be described as the voice of inexpressible fundamental existence, the mysterious knowledge of the *anima* (in contrast to the daylight knowledge of the *animus*), conscience (exceeding all knowledge and reflection) or the spark of light in the human soul. This knowledge is where freedom, knowledge and the Ego are as yet fused within that common root which must put forth its shoots to form the human personality. As a result of this light in the heart of our darkness, we always know who we are, but are unable to express it in words, even when confessing to God what we know of ourselves. Therefore, apart from the testimony of the Holy Ghost pleading within us " with unspeakable groanings," a man can only confess from the heart of his own darkness: " I am a sinner, O God. Have mercy on me." A man would cease to have any part of human existence were he to try to turn impatiently from his suffering, never knowing properly, never able to express his knowledge, never clearly realising what he is. He would cease to be himself did he try to observe and pass judgment on the actions of his life, like an impartial referee. For a man is himself involved in the actions he is attempting to judge. He can do nothing but run his race, and provided the direction of this race is away from self and towards God, he will soon cease to torture himself about the nature of that race. We are still on the course, and we must therefore forget what is behind us, even if the outcome of the race appears to have been already decided. Therefore the prayer which we must say concerning ourselves is never: " I am in Thy grace " but always: " Have mercy on me, a sinner." We can say these words in truth and in humility, because justification comes only through grace and because we never know whether we are justified, but only that justification is something beyond our unaided powers. The prayer of confession does not, of course, take on its full significance in isolation, any more than the fifth petition of the *Our Father* has a context other than that which places it in vital relation to the other petitions in that prayer. It is as united with the prayer of praise for the gift of God's love; with the prayer of thanksgiving for the living power of grace; with the prayer of hope; with the prayer for our necessities, and with unselfish prayer for our neighbour—that our prayer for forgiveness attains to the fulness of Christian prayer, in praise and glorification of God. Such a blending of prayer cannot be achieved by any process of reasoning. It is the free gift of the Holy Ghost.

VIII.

THE PRAYER OF DECISION.

" TIME travels in divers paces with divers people," says Shakespeare's Rosalind, and she goes on to list those " who Time ambles withal, who Time trots withal, who Time gallops withal, and who he stands still withal." Measured by the clock, one moment ticks over just as evenly as another; but as measured by the mind, an hour can live a minute, and a minute can seem like an hour. So, too, moments vary greatly in significance. There are dull moments when life just continues its monotonous flow, and there are burningly acute moments into which we feel that our whole past and all that we are is crowded, and which stand out in our lives as our moments of decision. Something is created in such a moment which shapes the course of our life irrevocably, or at least for a considerable period of time to come. Such moments do not begin and end in themselves; they, as it were, " look before and after," since the decision reached in them may well be determined by all that has gone before, and will certainly be made with a view to, or in defiance of, the future as thus determined. Thus, a whole life, and indeed eternity, may hang in the balance of such a moment. Hence, in the most literal sense they are the moments of decision.

The moment of choosing a career is an example of this; or that moment wherein we decide to link our life and destiny irrevocably with that of another person in Holy Matrimony. A marriage vow or a vow made to God is such a decision; and whoever takes it does so with a clear knowledge that, in the eyes of God, it is irrevocable, and may even be so too in the eyes of the law of the land. These, however, are the moments of public decision, announced with a certain amount of pomp and ceremony. Far more frequent, however, are those moments of decision which pass within a man's own mind, which no one witnesses. The straight path of one's years suddenly takes a bend, and, in the very heart of a routine existence, we are presented with a vital decision to be made—vital because on it depends the whole structure of our developing character, and because it is never likely to occur in the same way and with the same significance again. Life, or God, makes demands of us whether we will adhere to truth or take refuge in a cowardly falsehood; whether we will act justly or with unjust greed; whether we will choose the ennobling way of marital fidelity, or degrade our vow brutishly at the instigation of lust. The importance of such moments are to be measured, of course, by the importance and the consequences of the matter to be decided. There are some decisions which, as it were, just glance off the surface of a man's character; but there are others which reach down into his very foundations, so that, whether he shirks the decision of bravely meets it, one thing is certain—his character has been fundamentally affected for ill or for good.

It is to this latter kind that we especially refer when we speak about "moments of decision", for in them a man comes face to face with God. In such moments, a man is clearly aware of the answer demanded of him. He feels that the Hand of God has, as it were, been laid on him, and that the eyes of God are upon him asking whether the decision is to be that of selfishness or that dictated by the Will of God. It is God Who puts the question, and asks for His own reply on the lips and in the heart of a man. Thus the answer becomes a courageous crushing of the human will, an answer to the demands of Divine Love, a proof of a man's boundless confidences in the Will of God. On such decisions depends the very foundation of our relationship with God, for this relationship is essentially that of the loving oblation of the human will to the Divine Will. Hence the great significance for time and eternity of these moments of decision. They become moments of lived prayer, when a man chooses to make God's decision. They cannot be other than the very essence of prayer, since they are practical answers to the sweet insistence of Divine Love. Hence when we speak of the "prayer of decision," we mean that lived prayer in every decision made in accordance with the Will of God.

Let us consider three types of the prayer of decision:

prayer in temptation; the prayer of decision in our age; and the prayer of decision in the hour of death.

"Man's life on earth is a warfare," says Job; and no amount of wailing protest can alter that fact. We must accept temptation as part of human life, varying in matter and in intensity from man to man, but something very real for all of us. Temptation steals upon us unawares; we have no immunity for it, since it possesses as its powerful allies our own fallen nature, our thirst for human happiness, the eagerness of our senses to seek a glut of pleasure, or trust in the things of this world, our lack of living faith in the hereafter, and our amazing powers of self-deception in matters where a moral decision must be made. We can "sugar o'er the devil himself" by the ingenuity with which we put a face of goodness on our wickedness, so as to deceive not only others but even ourselves. This ingenuity reaches to the very principles of moral judgment, which we either blissfully ignore altogether, or set aside in favour of more "enlightened" standards of conduct formulated by ourselves. A stage is quickly reached when our conscience devises a kind of personal alchemy by which sin and perverse behaviour are transformed into virtue and righteousness.

Temptation, in the full sense of the word, is not a daily phenomenon in our lives, although, since the Scripture says that even the just man sins daily, each day will have its quota of minor temptations. However, as we use the term in this context, we mean that strong and decided temptation which assails us personally, and which seeks out the weak place in our spiritual defences. This does not mean, of course, that we must necessarily succumb, but it does mean that such temptations are a definite personal challenge to us which we must meet and answer as we should, if we are to grow in moral strength through conquering them. It would be deluded conceit for a man to imagine that his moral strength is all sufficient, or that he can marshal all his powers of resistance at any and every moment. He must, of course, have sufficient moral stamina to meet the sudden thrust of temptation; but he must also keep in mind that such stamina is not always at its best. Every man has troughs of weariness and depression, wherein even such vital considerations as God, life everlasting, virtue, truth, purity, and so forth, lose their lustre and their appeal and seem luxuries belonging to his happier states of mind. In such moods, pleasure, success, wealth and bodily comfort, take on an alluring appearance of palpable solidity; while the higher urges and the things of the spirit fade to a shadowy unreality, and concern about them seems but an elusive playing with shadows. This condition may be part of the temptation, in the sense it represents the gradual preparation for the assault.

Before openly attacking, temptation has infiltrated, after the manner of a fifth column, into the fortress of the soul, undermining its power of resistance. A condition is thus created in which it is possible for temptation to become very real and very dangerous for us. There will be no victory then, unless there is an increment of new moral strength in the very act of resisting. He who relies on his moral strength at the moment of being attacked, is bound to be eventually defeated. For he has already been cornered into a position of weakness by his love of comfort, his self-complacency and moral sloth. He is himself in league with the temptation. What, then, must he do? The spiritual significance of every great temptation is that by conquering it a man can add cubits to his moral stature; and he will arouse himself to do so, only by a vivid realisation through faith that his battle is on the plane of the eternal, not the temporal, and that eternity is the matter at stake. He must look up from his petty preoccupations, that strong spiritual winds may sweep his soul to strength. Faith must be his armour, and an intense love of God his spear and his shield. He must lift up the Divine Law in his own heart as a challenge to himself. Grace must sweep to the aid of free will, so that these two become a united strength wherein a man learns to brush from him with contempt the selfishness and love of pleasure, the weakness and the cowardice which have proved such insidious allies of the temptation. He must feel the strong surge of manly anger within him against that sophistry which attempts to falsify standards of conduct when they become awkward. He must scorn a heart which preferred comfort to constancy, fortune to fortitude, and its own will to the Will of its Creator. Only when he possesses such moral weapons is a man a true and efficient soldier of Christ, a warrior worthy of victory, standing prepared for the onslaught of any temptation. Thus armed, indeed, his victory is a foregone conclusion.

How are we to explain that moral miracle which occurs when a man whose inner spirit has been drab and slattern, is converted to God? Now a victim of his own crass presumption, and now a dupe of his own deluded conscience, such a man had ceased to know himself; and suddenly an Angel has placed a fiery sword in his hand, and the light and sweetness of God have taken possession of him. Such a sublime transformation will not take place, however, in one who meets a temptation languidly, who seeks to come to terms with temptation and is secretly resigned to defeat. Nor will it occur in one who seeks to delude himself into believing that there is some legitimate ground on which he and the temptation can come to an amicable settlement. The secret of such transformation is prayer, and prayer *only*. Suddenly beset with temptations to lust, weakness, cowardice, envy or despair, a man must summon all his strength of resistance, and must protest, with a strong cry to God, against his rebellious flesh and his temporising mind. He must not seek to fight unaided, but must turn with all the urgency of his heart to God. He must fly from his own weakness to the strength of God; from his own wavering infidelity to the eternal changelessness of God. He must beg for love, plead for the gift of the Holy Ghost, thirst for the strength that comes from Christ dying on the Cross. The grace given in answer to such prayer will alone give courage to relinquish his hunger for the pleasures of this world, and choose the way of justice and of Divine Truth. He must not parley and reason with the temptation, but must plead with God; and in making this plea, he must not concern himself with the temptation, but only with the Grace, the Life, the Love, of which he knows himself to be so vitally in need.

Nothing pleases the tempting serpent so much as a man's willingness to discuss the whole matter with him, for the serpent knows that a man's poor brain is no match for his own cunning. To get a man to consider nicely the law against which he is tempted, to make a subtle distinction about its application in this or that particular set of circumstances, is already a victory for the tempter. A man must therefore turn from all this, and fix his mind on God, the only sure and everlasting foundation, the adorable First Principle of all moral principles. Only through prayer can we overcome temptation, because only through prayer can a man regain that holy innocence of the children of God which instinctively rejects and despises the enticement of sin. Real temptation always finds us weaker than we should be; otherwise, our inclinations and the lower cravings of our nature would not be so ready to ally themselves with the temptation. The conquest of temptation is, therefore, the conquest of these inclinations and cravings, through a returning of our hearts to a full allegiance to God and through pleading for His assistance.

We must pray in temptation, and we must learn how really to pray. Let us never say in temptation: " I cannot resist "; let us rather turn with renewed faith and revived love to God, and say: " I know that Thou canst save me." Let us not say despairingly to ourselves: " I cannot live without this pleasure or that posssession "; let us rather lift our voice in an earnest, persistent, reiterated prayer: " Lord, without *Thee* I cannot live." Let us not say to our dark oppressive weakness: " You are my death "; but: " You are the dawn of my true life which must begin in a realisation of my own weakness." Remember the warning of Saint Augustine: " Do not darken thy darkness; God doth not darken it, but rather enlighteneth it." We must cry for that enlightenment which will prevent us from being deceived by a temper disguised as an angel of light. We must not listen to a thousand specious reasons why, in this particular case, the law of God does not apply, nor to flattering arguments about the law's being designed for people less enlightened than we are. Let us pray for protection against what has been called " the mysticism of sin," to which Saint Paul was referring when he said: " Should we continue in sin that grace may abound? God forbid." (*Romans* 6:1). The grace of God can raise a poor sinner from his fall; but woe to him who, having fallen, does not believe that God is greater than his sin, and to the even less enlightened person who permits himself to fall in order that God may have the opportunity of raising him again! He is guilty of presumption in taking for granted beforehand that God will do so. There are sins against the Holy Ghost which are forgiven neither in this life nor in the next. A person who deliberately wishes to be redeemed by sinning and being raised from his sin, is dangerously close to the sin against the Holy Ghost; and, at the present time, it is to be feared that this temptation lays hold of many. Let us always pray for enlightenment in our temptations.

We must cultivate a sensitivity to the first signs of internal weakness and loss of spiritual vigour. That inner feeling of well-being which is associated with spiritual and mental health, begins to give place to ill-humour, to irritability, and to a distaste for spiritual things (*acedia*). The love of God grows weak in us, and His yoke becomes bitter where before it was sweet. Our sensitivity of conscience must sound the warning, and we must immediately set about retrieving the spiritual ground we have lost. Calmly and without anxiety, we must attempt to reestablish that interior harmony which has become disrupted. It is even more imperative that we should do so when it was a temptation which first drew our attention to the weakened state of our spiritual life. More than ever, it is then our duty to turn earnestly to God.

Only by keeping close to God can we escape the pervasive power of evil, which would otherwise slowly poison heart, mind and soul. There can be no victory for him who, while he does not actually accept defeat, is yet unwilling to shake off the sluggishness of his heart. He fails to recognise the true nature of temptation as an invitation to take a more firm grasp on the love of God. The answer to this invitation is prayer—prayer in all its forms.

If a person is subjected to a continuous onslaught of evil thoughts and desires, it may be as well for him to refrain from praying explicitly for deliverance from this temptation. To pray explicitly for this, might result in fixing his mind all the more on the temptation, thus aggravating his condition. His prayer should be characterised by a cheerful trust in God, and by quiet perseverance; for this will enable him to ignore the obsessive thoughts and desires by bravely throwing himself into the business of his daily life. Such strategy of spiritual warfare means looking to God for strength; and this is prayer.

Temptation is a moment of decision, and victory is dependent on prayer. Our Lord said: "Watch ye and pray that ye enter not into temptation" (*Math.* 26:41). Prayer in temptation is the prayer of decision.

Let us briefly consider the second type of prayer of decision: that in our own age, which age is a moment of decision to a far greater degree than were other periods in human history. Many things have already been decided. Europe, once chosen by God to bring the Name of Christ to the nations of the whole earth, has lost the leadership of the world. Its strength has been undermined by its own infidelity. Having rent the seamless garment of Christian unity, it went on to adore the golden calf of material progress, adopted rationalism as its new faith, and was abandoned to the horrors of its own blind tyranny, the swastika taking the place of the Cross. Europe has forfeited its right to lead, and therefore God's command and the honour attaching to that command seem about to be transferred to other nations and other races, who will one day bring forth fruits more worthy of the Kingdom of God—though, indeed, at the present moment, it would be difficult to point out any nation which would seem to qualify for this great destiny.

Decisions have been taken, in which is revealed, through what seem the iron laws of history, the bitter-sweet severity of Divine Love guiding the course of mankind. We have witnessed developments which have taken place in accordance with their own inexorable laws. In the course of these developments and these decisions, certain opportunities have occurred, either to be seized upon or ignored; and such opportunity may recur. Europe may be given a breathing space in which to realise how it has failed in its God-given mission, and how possibilities of further evil or new blessing depend on whether it awakens to a sense of its new responsibilities. If indeed it does so, God may give it a new soul to work for the spread of His Kingdom—may reinvest it with its ancient dignity as His ambassadors, His special family of nations. On this depends not only the happiness of Europe itself, but the personal happiness of each and every European.

As yet, it is impossible to say whether Europe, like the precious box of alabaster (Mark, 14:3) is destined to be broken in order that the fragrance of its faith, its spirit and its history may pervade the whole world; or whether it will simply be broken as a vessel gone sour and useless, and its shards flung aside by the potter as worthy only of the dustbin. It is yet an open question whether God will give the nations of Europe, beloved by Him from the dawn of Christianity, another period of peace so that they may regain their lost sense of a Christian vocation to the whole world; or whether, having failed in that mission, these nations may degenerate into physical and spiritual paupers. Must Europe become again the battlefield of the world, and collapse in a final ruin of blood and tears, before a new era is ushered in? But who can read the Mind of God? Or who can be His counsellor?

Yet, there is one thing which emerges quite clearly. Despite the alleged dictates of so-called historical determinism, by whose laws God is not bound, God can still say to the nations of Europe what He said to the people of His Old Dispensation: Behold, today I place before you life and happiness, or death and misfortune. I call upon the heavens and the earth to witness that today I have put before you life or death, blessing or a curse. Choose therefore life, that life may remain with you and with your seed. Love the Lord your God; obey Him and remain true to Him. Your life depends on the choice you make . . . That choice we have still to make, and there are many false roads to which we are being beckoned. But the decision is ours to make.

We stand among the ruined years, but we can still claim our right. We can still find courage to pray for the happiness and the true greatness of Europe. Through His Blessed Mother, the Lord has urged us to pray for this intention; and such prayer will be a real force in determining the story of Europe today, and the future of the world. Are we going to obey Him? Are we going to become a great family of praying Christian nations—each earnestly imploring a renaissance of grace, each pleading for the rebirth of Europe as the continent of God, however desperate that plea may seem? Will our prayer be the prayer of our faith in God's omnipotence, or our hope when, humanly speaking, hope seems dead? Or will we remain hardened and disillusioned, indifferent and selfish, concerned only with rescuing our own few sticks from the general conflagration, and callous about what happens to our neighbours—obedient to that dictum of Hell that " now is it every man for himself "? The general obligation of prayer in this crisis is laid upon all alike, and there will be no prayer if every man waits for his neighbour to begin, in accordance with that other principle one hears so much nowadays that " it is as much his duty as mine." Are we going to become victims of that herd instinct by which the individual recognises his duty only when that duty has become socially accepted in practice, and no longer demands anything of him except to take the direction of the herd? Our age is one of vital historical decisions affecting the whole of mankind: it is unique in that every such decision has its repercussions from pole to pole. Does this situation bring us to our knees in ardent prayer that these decisions may in accordance with the infinitely merciful Will of God?

The third type of prayer of decision we have listed above, is that in the hour of death. The whole life of a man is gathered into that hour, and his past appears clear, solid and final at that moment when for him time is to be swallowed up in eternity. In the hour of death, both God and the dying person speak their last word—a word which is final and decisive for all eternity. The important question for us is whether we shall obtain the grace to make our last conscious moment a moment filled with the prayer of decision, by which we mean such a prayer as will lift up all that we were and are, all we have done and suffered, in oblation to the mercy of God; whether, as the shades of death darken in our minds, we shall turn a last glance of faith on Him Who has crossed the bar of death and yet behold He lives. Shall we say to Him at that moment: " Come, Lord Jesus "; and will that prayer be strengthened by the prayer of the *Sponsa Christi*, the " prayer of faith " (James 5:15) spoken by the minister of His Church anointing us to appear before the King of Everlasting Life? Shall we be able to pray in that hour of decision, to commend our souls into the hands of God? May God mercifully grant us the grace to depart from this world in prayer, so that the last thought in our minds may fit us for life everlasting. Blessed is he who can utter a prayer of decision when the hour comes which is for him the most decisive of all.

We do not know whether we shall be given the grace to meet death with full consciousness, greeting it with prayer and resignation as the messenger of God. For death comes like a thief in the night. We have no assurance that our last word of decision on time and eternity will not be spoken at a moment when we do not think that death is at hand. Therefore we must begin in time to tend the lamp of our faith and our love, that it may always be filled with the oil of good works. Let us watch and pray, so that the Lord at His coming may not find us asleep. That prayer of decision which we wish to say in the hour of our death must be said by us again and again during our life. We must pray now for the decision of that future hour, and we must pray for the grace of fortitude. Let us pray that God may prevent us from being separated from Him, and that even when we are about to leave Him, He will not leave us, but lovingly compel our wayward heart back into His service, through His almighty and mysteriously gentle grace. To think of one's death is prayer indeed, a prayer of decision. The uncertainty of the hour of death compels us to anticipate in our everyday prayer, the prayer for the hour of death. Our everyday prayer thus becomes an intimate preparation for the ultimate prayer of decision. Let us pray unceasingly.

We have said much—perhaps in too many words—about the subject of prayer. And yet, we have said almost nothing, and many points of importance have scarcely been touched. One point above all should have been made in and for our age. The prophet Isaias stated an essential prerequisite for true prayer when he said (58 : 7 and 9): "Deal thy bread to the hungry and bring the needy and the harbourless into thy house, then thou shalt call and the Lord shall hear. Thou shall cry and he shall say: I am here." What we can say *about* prayer is of little consequence: what matters is what we say *in* prayer. These words we find for ourselves. They may be shy, weak and poor; they may rise on silver wings to the heavens from a cheerful heart; or they may be drawn with pain from the deep wells of sorrow. They may have in them a resonance like thunder among the hills; or they have in them the softness of summer rain. What matters only is that they come from our heart, and that we desire our hearts to be raised to God with them.

What matters is that the spirit of God lives in our prayer. Such prayer is heard by God. No word of such prayer will be forgotten. For God will give an answer of love to prayers which come to him in words of warm sincerity. That answer will be the giving of Himself to us at every moment of our lives, and most of all in that last hour of decision, when "the shadows lengthen, and the evening comes, and the busy world is hushed, and the fever of life is over, and our work is done. Then in His mercy may He give us a safe lodging and a holy rest, and peace at last!" (Cardinal Newman).

This "safe lodging," this "holy rest," this "peace at last," will be the reward of our fidelity in prayer.